Let's Go to Play Golf

Let's Go to Play Golf

발 행 | 2024년 7월 30일
저 자 | 김한갑
펴낸이 | 한건희
펴낸곳 | 주식회사 부크크
출판사등록 | 2014.07.15.(제2014-16호)
주 소 | 서울특별시 금천구 가산디지털1로 119 SK트윈타워 A동 305호
전 화 | 1670-8316
이메일 | info@bookk.co.kr

ISBN | 979-11-410-9814-8

www.bookk.co.kr

Let's Go
to Play Golf

HANKAP KIM

Preface

We started learning English in middle schools and continued to learn it for more than 10 years through high schools and colleges, and yet we are experiencing the misfortune of having to start learning English again because we cannot speak English fluently when we go out into the social society.

This is because language is not a theory. It can only be mastered by speaking it step by step through everyday conversation in our daily life.

The same goes true for golf. Golf is not a theory. It is a practice. Golf skills can only be mastered by actually shaking the club every day in practice rather than in theory.

This is not to say that theory is not necessary for golf, but theory is only a guideline and standard. Therefore in order to learn the essence of golf, you must master the technique by hitting thousands and thousands of balls to be able to play golf and enjoy the fun of it.

Now It is more than two decades since the turn of the century and it is no exaggeration to say that the golf world has not only changed significantly during these decades, but also has fundamentally transformed in its essence, with many young people participating a completely new world of golf. There has never been a time in my life when so many things have changed and developed so rapidly.

At this point, when the popularization of golf has progressed so greatly, the globalization of golf has also progressed greatly, and it is now inevitable that our citizens will go out into the world and make friends with many foreigners in the future.

Therefore, golf books in English have also been requested widely, so that many young people can read them. I worked hard to ensure that there would be no inconvenience for young people in playing with foreigners when going abroad. So, I sincerely hope that young people go abroad, socialize with foreign people and by playing golf, have fun and experience the wide world.

That's why I wrote this book. In actual golf, many different people produce different swings and strokes. No two persons have the same swing. Even for the same person, the results are different from day to day. In this respect, golf can be said to be a practical stroke that applies and adapts basic skills according to the changes in specific situations.

In that sense, golfing can be said to be a difficult path and a challenging process in which one learns each skill day by day in practice rather than thousands of theories.

And so regardless of their motivations to play golf, many people who start playing golf go through trial and error just like everyone else. This is the same experience whether you are a professional or an amateur.

However, those who want to become professionals must learn the principles quickly by training themselves harder and harder and more systematically, while amateurs practice as much as time allows, otherwise they have no choice but to fall behind in many ways through trial and error.

Even among amateurs, there would be quite a few people who would have achieved great success if they had set their feet on the golfing field in early years and turned professional.

Therefore, this book is intended to shorten practical experience for amateur golfers who do not have enough time and leisure to learn all the advanced techniques like professionals, and to develop their skills by describing various field experiences not covered in general technique textbooks.

It's been more than 50 years since I picked up a golf club, and I'm now in my senior years. I hope that this small book will serve as a guide for the younger generation so that they can improve their skills as soon as possible and enjoy the pleasure of golf.

June 2024
Hankap Kim

Contents

1. The Battle of Armageddon

As the end of the Earth approaches, we are told that a grand epic unfolds before us, where good and evil will finally battle in Armageddon to determine the winner. So It becomes a battlefield of cruel fate, shedding blood as if it were the final judgment.

From the beginning, neither side wins unilaterally, but the wins and losses are mixed, creating a panorama that makes you sweat. When the battle is over, the winner becomes good and the loser becomes evil.

In a golf match, not only is the battle for the lead over four days so intense that it is difficult to determine who is superior, but it is also a breath-taking decisive battle until the very last moment of the final day.

When it comes to the world famous major champion tournaments, a nail-biting battle takes place with people around the world watching. Thus, the final winner holds the victory trophy high and cheers, while the loser remains silent.

A. Greg Norman's Tragedy

In the 1989 British Open, Greg Norman was one stroke ahead of his opponent Calcavecchia, after two holes in a play-off that went into overtime in the fourth round.

On the third 223-yard short hole, Greg Norman's ball crossed the green to the apron and Calcavechia cleared it. Even though it was the apron, Greg Norman was one point ahead, so he could have made par. However, Greg Norman used his unique technique to hit the ball into the hole for a birdie, but the ball passed the hole and was too far away to get par.

At this time, the ball Calcavecchia hit almost went into the hole, but he caught par just a little short of the hole. Greg Norman eventually missed par and ended up with bogey, so the scores of the two were tied.

In the fourth and final 452-yard hole, Greg Norman's ball flew straight to the front of the fairway but flew to the right and fell into a cross bunker.

Meanwhile, Calcavecchia's ball curved to the right, but hit the crowd and ended up in the fairway. Afterwards, Greg Norman's ball, which he hit from the bunker, fell into the bunker again, and the ball he hit from there entered the gravel field, resulting in a loss of points. Calcavecchia at last had achieved a come-from-behind victory with two ons, bringing the day's match to its finale.

I think that the match on this day was because Greg Norman was too greedy to increase the score by not keeping the points earned up to 2 holes. Greg Norman, who was hitting in good conditions that day, may not have decided to hit a normal hit.

Greg Norman was so motivated to do his best with each stroke and hit a famous hit that would go down in history, so that he tried to use a shot that would never back down, but he collapsed on the fourth and final hole.

Why is it that Greg Norman was weak in overtime and had a win-loss ratio of 2:7 until his last time? Not only is his win rate low compared to his reputation, but he has not achieved great results in major tournaments despite being number one in the rankings?

He usually maintained an overwhelming lead through the first, second, and third rounds, but collapsed in the last fourth rounds and lost the championship.

Tall height, sharp eyes, a patented great white shark hat, and an exciting tee shot. What was lack with him?

It's definitely refreshing to see a match in which he appears. Is it just that? When he takes the lead, you can enjoy the thrill of watching.

And when Greg Norman's putt didn't go in, the son's gesture of breaking up and hitting the ground seemed like the whole family was creating a panorama. However, despite his high popularity and ranking, Greg Norman was weak in major tournaments.

From our perspective, Greg Norman appears to be a technical player who feels more joy in hitting each shot perfectly and making the right shot at the right time, rather than focusing on the total score and wanting to win the championship.

Otherwise, wouldn't it be too cunning for him to refrain from playing a game where you can sometimes hit a safe shot with a spoon or iron rather than a driver and hit the ball defensively?

There was a time when he was worried about not hitting a good shot, and he received a coach to make corrections and learned oriental Zen philosophy to get psychological adjustment.

But isn't it said that golf is a game of skills occupying only 30$ out of total victory? No matter how good your technique is, if your mental stability is broken and you feel psychological anxiety, the ball will not go as you want. In addition, no matter how well you hit the ball, the lie of the ball is difficult, so in many cases it is extremely difficult to hit the next shot.

Therefore, wouldn't it be difficult to achieve a perfect score of 288 in 4 rounds? There is no way he does not know this simple truth, but the tragic man Greg Norman always disappoints the spectators at the end and makes them feel sad.

The world's best golfer, Greg Norman, is like this, but even more so when it comes to us amateur golfers. For example, players around us who are said to be pretty good at hitting a ball in the rough, topping it with a wood when there are still 200 yards left, or imitating Fred Couples and hitting the ground with a great swing, etc. There are many cases where you get bogged down while trying to hit a perfect shot. Should you take the risk and aim for a perfect shot, or should you play safely with the next best shot? It's worth thinking about at least once.

B. Gil Morgan's Self-Destruction

Gil Morgan. In the 1992 when US Open was held at Pebble Beach on the west coast of the United States, he showed good performance in the first and second rounds, taking the lead, and stood out by recording a 9 under par at the end of the second round, 4 strokes clear of the follow-up player.

In the third round, he continued to lead until the first 7 holes, widening the gap by 7 points over the runner-up with 12 under par, and it looked like he was solidifying his position as champion. However, since it is a beach, the weather can change drastically, so nobody did know what would happen.

The problem was that on the 8th middle hole, the ball on his second shot fell into a bunker and started to go out of alignment in an instant. From there, he started to shake and recorded double bogey, bogey, double bogey, bogey, etc. in a row, losing most of the golden scores he had earned over three days before.

Because others were also busy maintaining the status quo, and only a few people making under-par, made it difficult to gauge the results.

Tom Kite was among them. He had been unlucky in major tournaments so far, but this time, the ball he approached from the fringe chipped in, hinting at good fortune.

On the last day, the trophy went to Tom Kite with a 3-under par, and Gil Morgan had no choice but to suffer bitter hardship.

When we watch a game like this, we wonder if great players can collapse so easily, we can't help but wonder what the cause was.

In fact, professionals have to be physically very strong because they compete for four days. Also, even if you are physically strong, it is common for each person to use their own unique physical training method to maintain their physical strength for four days.

And since there are differences in sleeping, eating, and leisure use, it can be seen that this affects the game resulting in different results for each round.

Therefore, it can be said that it is customary to prepare in advance in order to maintain the best condition for major competitions. Gary Player writes in his autobiography that when he leaves the house before a game, he feels refreshed and somehow feels like he is going to win today, then the result is good.

Therefore, if you fail to maintain your physical condition or are constantly stressed due to complications at home, your golf game will not go well and you will feel like you are going back and forth to hell, unlike yesterday.

In 1996, Greg Norman, who was also unlucky in major tournaments, maintained the lead from the beginning through the first, second, and third rounds at the Masters in the United States, raising the interest of spectators as they wondered if he would win the Masters this time. However, in the 4th round, he collapsed and lost the championship. It was a pity.

Tiger Woods, known as a golf prodigy, also turned professional in the fall of 1996 and, in his third appearance at the Quad City Classic, hit a long shot that made his comeback through the third round, killing the spirit of the existing professionals and leaving the gallery in awe. However, he also lost his chance to win by falling to over par in the 4th round.

Seeing world-class players collapsing like this, it may be impossible for amateurs to play a complete game from start to finish. In that respect, I don't think there is anything to be discouraged even if your score is not good.

Of course, amateur golfers in Korea usually finish the game in one day even if it is a weekend or weekday, so they are different from professionals who maintain their condition for three or four days.

However, even in a long-awaited class reunion or a game where co-workers gather to compete to show off their skills, it will be difficult to get a good score if you do not condition yourself a few days in advance.

Additionally, amateur golf matches do not involve major interests, and the main purpose is often social networking and gatherings, so there is no need to be upset even if your score is bad. Wouldn't it be fun to keep practicing your swing again to get a good score next time?

연도	Masters	US Open	British Open	PGA Championship
87	Larry Mize	Scott Simpson	Nick Faldo	Larry Nelson
88	Sandy Lyle	Curtis Strange	Seve Ballesteros	Jeff Sluman
89	Nick Faldo	Curtis Strange	Mark Calcavecchia	Payne Stewart
90	Nick Faldo	Hale Irwin	Nick Faldo	Wayne Grady
91	Ian Woosnam	Payne Stewart	Ian Baker-Finch	John Daly
92	Fred Couples	Tom Kite	Nick Faldo	Nick Price
93	Bernhard Langer	Lee Janson	Greg Norman	Paul Azinger
94	Jose Maria Olazabal	Ernie Els	Nick Price	Nick Price
95	Ben Crenshaw	Corey Pavin	John Daly	Steve Elkington
96	Nick Faldo	Steve Jones	Tom Lehman	Mark Brooks

Major Champions in the Last Decades of Last Century

C. John Daly and Corey Pavin

John Daly appeared like a comet in 1991 and won the US PGA Championship with long hits. After that, he won the British Open in 1995 with a swing and form that no one could imitate, and has been talked about by people, making him a hot topic and being evaluated as the Ten Million Dollar Man.

In comparison, when Corey Pavin, who was short in stature and seemingly frail, won the US Open in 1995 with an accurate shot as if measured by a ruler and an approach shot close to the hole, the world once again enjoyed the pleasure of golf. Long—hitting John Daly or short—hitting Corey Pavin, which will golfer choose?

Of course, it goes without saying that an accurate long hit is advantageous, but in a golf game where the tee shot is not everything, an accurate approach shot and the accuracy of putting on the green do not necessarily require strength alone, so many long hitters usually win awards, but It is also common to lose control and be defeated by an experienced short player.

Soon after starting to learn golf, almost everyone puts in every effort to improve distance.

However, except for a few people who are born with a natural ability or who have developed an athletic sense through sports such as tennis or baseball, isn't it normal for most people to worry about slices or hooks and not be able to achieve distance?

In Korea, golf beginners usually start practicing with driver shots. Whether it's right or wrong.

When you are trying to swing the longest pole and hit the target when you can't move your body properly or see the ball clearly, it would be as difficult as someone born in the city going down to the countryside and swinging a flail during the harvest season.

In most cases, when men or women start learning golf as a hobby in their 20s or 30s, the distance the ball flies can be determined to some extent by the person's waist movement and wrist strength. So shouldn't you practice hitting straight at first?

Of course, some instructors argue that the ball should be sent far away at first. In particular, if Koreans want to advance into the world and compete with tall foreigners, they cannot hope to become champions without hitting the same long shots as them. Actually it is.

However, not everyone can hit a long ball. Even among pros, there are not many who can hit over 270 yards on average. What would be the result if Corey Pavin, who can only hit to fly 250 yards, tried to throw 300 yards to match John Daly? No doubt, some of them got into the rough, and then lost the scores he had earned, and fell out of the winning ranks.

Also, John Daly does not always hold the driver to hit tee shots. Sometimes he try to hit the tee shot with a spoon or a long iron and hit it accurately. Moreover, golf courses usually have long courses and short courses, and some are wide and some are narrow. I believe that the way to victory is to change clubs depending on the time and place and hit accurately. There is no need to be disappointed just because you are a short hitter.

Recently, with the development of golf tools and techniques, the number of players who can hit the ball accurately while hitting it far has increased. Especially as new players who hit accurate long shots are increasing, the choice between long and short hits is not an issue, but rookies who play in a balanced manner by harmonizing the two methods are also increasing, and a new era of golf is unfolding.

It's not about whether it's John Daly or Corey Pavin, but golf is constantly evolving as new hitting methods and new tools are constantly being developed and new players who are learning them are emerging in order to hit more accurately and farther.

D. Match play and stroke play

The game enjoyed by amateur golfers in Korea consists of at least an 18-hole regular round stroke play, in which the player who plays the least strokes wins. And match play, in which the winner of each hole is determined with the smallest strokes, is played between close friends.

Of course, stroke play and match play each have different types of playing methods, but fundamentally stroke play is based on the total of strokes after the round, whereas match play determines win or loss for each hole, so there is a difference in the way they are played.

In general, stroke play is based on the total number of strokes, so you need to hit well, but you also need to prevent over-par such as bogeys or double bogeys by preventing mishits. Even if you hit several holes well, you can hit triple bogeys or worse in one or two holes in following holes. Then your recovery is difficult.

In contrast, in match play, the winner or loser is decided at each hole, so you must aim for a birdie or par. So If you hit a bad shot and lose that hole by hitting a double bogey or triple bogey, it will not affect the calculation of the winning or losing for the next holes.

In recent professional competitions, due to the spread of commercialism, the stroke play method has been adopted to select one winner with a huge prize money, and competitions between countries and regions where honor is at stake, such as the Ryder Cup or Presidents Cup, are decided by the stroke plays. Sometimes It combines stroke play and match play formats.

And the so-called skins game, in which several famous players are invited to compete against each other, usually uses the match play method.

Of course, someone who is good at stroke play can also be good at match play, but compared to stroke play, match play requires much more challenging play and adds the element of luck, which makes it more interesting.

And while stroke play focuses on a stable

score, match play focuses on the hole rather than the final score and takes on a bold challenge, so it can be said to be a method worth trying for young golfers with a lot of potential in the future.

However, because the win or loss is determined by the match between holes, there is a gambling element depending on the cost of winning or losing, and it is considered taboo in our society.

In general, compared to older golfers whose swings are stable due to long experience and practice and whose scores are not subject to severe ups and downs, but who have little motivation to further improve their skills, the young golfers have the potential to improve in the future and so need to hone their skills more. Regardless of the score of the round that day. It would be a good idea to actively seize opportunities and try new techniques, aiming for a single handy next time and trying the match play too in the coming next days.

2. Golf prodigy Tiger Woods and changes in the golf world

At the turn of century, a giant new genius of golf appeared in this world and raised wide sensation around the world.

And so the golf world too changed much in every aspects of golf field such as prize money and field structures, and people's participation into the golf world expanded so much. So he, in a sense, contributed so much to the expansion and techniques of the golf world, but Tiger Woods was not so happy. He had been puzzled with various accidents and almost stopped to play golf, only hoping his child grows succeeding him in the future.

We at first should recognize his accomplishments in the golfing world and then we should do analyze why he should have to fail to live in human life lately.

A. The emergence of golf prodigy Tiger Woods

Golf has been a gambling event for white people for a long time. Since it has been established as a good sports in Scotland, it's been played only in the high society, but since it's been imported Into the United States, black persons were effectively banned from golf courses, and blacks have been openly criticized by the whites saying that they should serve as caddies only.

Against this trend of the old time, black pioneers, especially Charlie Sifford and Lee Elder, boldly took on the challenge and won some of the championships, and continued their efforts by advocating for the improvement of the status of blacks and their joining the PGA, which was finally achieved in 1995. And so It became possible for black people to join the golf club of PGA.

Meanwhile, Tiger's father, Earl Woods, a former member of the US Air Force, married a Thai woman in Thailand and gave birth to Tiger Woods in 1975. It is said that he recognized Woods' talent from an early age and began formally teaching him golf when he was only 4 years old. Tiger, born with talent for golf, showed off his talent from an early age. He won the US Junior Amateur Golf Tournament in succession three times from 1991, and Amateur Championship three times from 1994, and received a golf scholarship from Stanford University. However, in 1996, he dropped out of the university and registered with the PGA to officially pursue golf thereafter.

His performance after that was dazzling. Tiger Woods, who was 1m 88cm tall and has a slim physique weighing 70kg, was already the champion of the US Junior Amateur Championship before turning to pro in August 1996.

Of the seven tournaments held during the 50 days of his professional debut, he won two tournaments, the Las Vegas Invitational and the Walt Disney Classic, and jumped to 23rd place in the US PGA Tour prize money rankings.

Tiger Woods' golf talent was revealed in many places. He ranked 60th at the Milwaukee Open, a pro debut tournament, but after that, he showed amazing records of 11th, 5th, 3rd, 1st, 3rd, and 1st, and the average number of strokes per round was 67.89. In addition, in the two major competitions, Las Vegas and Walt Disney Classic, he defeated two of prominent mid-generation players by beating Davis Love III and Payne Stewart respectively.

Then, in 1997, he became the Mercedes champion, and in April he finally won the long-awaited major tournament, the Masters tournament, breaking all records and becoming a huge star, causing a tectonic shift in the golf world.

He was clearly a golf prodigy who was attracting attention since he had the talent to improve with further refinement, including an exciting driver shot of 322.6 yards, which was far ahead of John Daly's tee shot distance at the Las Vegas Classic, and a flexible approach and putting sense.

The emergence of golf prodigy Tiger Woods was not a coincidence, however. As golf became popular at the end of the 20th century, it was becoming a new phenomenon that players with talent in golf were distinguishing themselves at a much younger age than before.

Recently in the turn of the century, young players such as Phil Michaelson, Tim Hereon, and Justin Leonard have stood out on the American stage, and young players such as Seongjae Lim are creating a sensation in Korea as well. Unlike the past, it can be said that the period has come for the younger generation to advance into the golf world far ahead of the old generation.

Therefore, the fact that there are many parents in Korea who are working hard to teach their children on golf at an early age and is expected to brighten the future of our life in golf.

However, prodigies sometimes do not go long. In that respect, if you do not practice consistently by accumulating practical experience based on your innate talent, you may be overtaken by a new prodigy and your life will not be goring long, and you may become frustrated, so you need to continue to train yourself.

Comparison of Big golfers at their 1st year

(순위)

Tiger Woods(1996)		Jack Nicklaus(1962)		Arnold Palmer(1955)	
Milwaukee Open	T60	L. A. Open	T50	Phoenix	T10
Canadian Open	11	San Diego	T15	Tucson	T44
Quad City Classic	T 5	Bing Crosby	T23	Texas Open	T 6
B. C. Open	T 3	Lucky Int'l	T47	Houston	T22
Las Vegas intal	1	Palm Springs	T32	Baton Rouge	T41
Texas Open	3	Phoenix	T 2	St. Petersburg	T18
Walt Disney Classic	1	New Orleans	T17	Miami Beach	T21

B. Tiger's major wins

In 2000, Tiger's best season ever, he recorded a total of 26 under par in eight weekend rounds of the four major tournaments. From the late 1990s until the 2010s, Tiger won successively with a fierceness that other players could not even think of chasing him. He used to hold the trophy in his hands.

Before 2009, out of a total of 94 rounds of major tournaments in which Tiger participated, there were 39 cases where Tiger scored under par by 70 strokes. What an incredible record, considering that it is a major tournament where one can aim for the win even with a total score of over par for all four rounds.

However, in the major tournaments he participated in after that, out of 26 weekend rounds, he recorded a tie of under 70 just three times. Until 2013, there were no opportunities for him to win additional major championships. In 20 major tournaments since 2009, Tiger has recorded top 10 scores nine times, and among them, he has achieved excellent results by finishing in the top four six times.

But Tiger's 15th major victory now seemed far away due to his poor performance in the final round. His continued injuries and subsequent decline in stamina was the problem. It is true that even in 2018, when he successfully returned from injury, his chances of winning seemed low because he did not show the same charisma as in the past in the 3rd and 4th rounds of major competitions when he was in the past championship bracket.

However, in the 2019 Masters Tournament, he entered the final round two strokes behind the leader, and won with a record of 2 under par in the fourth round following 5 under par in the third round, achieving the great feat of 'comeback victory in a major tournament' for the first time in his career. He achieved it. He announced his health to golf fans around the world with a valuable victory that erased his long slump in the 3rd and 4th rounds.

By 2008, Tiger had won a total of 14 major championships and was the only player to win more than all of them. However, after being dealt with an unexpected blow by Yang Yong-Eun at the 2009 PGA Championship, the tremendous charisma and performance he showed in his 14 wins was not felt.

So, he changed swing coaches four times, but the results were not satisfactory. The only notable results were Tiger's injury and Major's continued failure. Tiger's nervousness must have felt like pressure as the major rounds escalated due to lack of results amid various changes of health conditions. Although he worked hard to win, Tiger is likely to continue his career as a player with less confidence than before by the passage of time and his body constantly breaking down.

For Tiger, who is in his mid-40s and suffering from serious injuries that make his everyday life uncomfortable, hoping for a miracle of winning his 15th major seemed like a pretty unreasonable request. So 2018, in which many injuries were corrected, ended as a year in which an answer to the 'unreasonable demand' of achieving a 15th major was expected. He showed enough performance to raise expectations that he might get his 15th major victory.

After competing for the championship in The Open, he finished in 6th place and in 2nd place in the PGA Championship, and the Tour Championship, the last game of the 'playoffs'. Everybody hoped to see his spectacular comeback by winning his 80th career win. Afterwards, he lost the $10 million event against Phil Mickelson due to a failure to control his knee and other conditions, and placed almost last in a competition hosted by his foundation.

And yet at the Masters Tournament held in April 2019 next year, he won his 5th Masters championship, his first major championship in 11 years. It was his 15th major win, and although it still won't be easy, he has begun his journey to match Jack Nicklaus' record of 18 major wins?

Tiger's Major Memories

....

1997	Masters Tournament
1999	PGA Championship
2000	US Open
2000	The Open Championship
2000	PGA Championship_2nd Time
2001	Masters Tournament_2nd Time
2002	Masters Tournament_3rd Time
2002	US Open_2nd Time
2005	Masters Tournament_4th Time
2005	The Open Championship_2nd Time
2006	The Open Championship_3rd Time
2008	US Open_3rd Time
2019	Masters Tournament 5th Time

C. Tiger's style of play

Tiger Woods said. "People judged me as stupid for trying to change the swing that gave me so many wins in the majors. They even asked me why I was changing my swing. But I believed that only through these changes could I develop myself further."

As Tiger recalled, he took the unprecedented path of correcting his swing when he was in the top, and did so twice. However, he came out on top with a completely changed swing. After changing his swing, he returned to the field and commanded the world every time, and through this, he re-entered the top prize money and Player of the Year titles.

Tiger was the first golfer to show that he could dominate the field with long shots, and it was he who started the trend of focusing on fitness to hit long shots. There are some opinions that too much muscle exercise caused the injury, but there are cases like Rory Mcilroy, so it has not been clearly proven yet. However, it is true that long shots bring money, so after Tiger, it has become difficult to become a top player if he does not know how to hit over 300 yards with a driver. There has never been a case like Tiger that showed that long shots are essential for victory.

Tiger's performance at the 1997 Masters Tournament shocked and inspired many at the time. Before that, there were players like Jack Nicklaus who hit close to 300 yards with an actual 'wood' driver, and there were players like John Daly who opened the era of 'average season distance of 300 yards', but there was no case that directly demonstrated this like Tiger, saying 'long shots are essential for victory'.

Tiger's play style of sending a long shot and hitting the pin with a short iron for the second shot has had a great influence, and now everyone is playing with a similar strategy. So now some of the golf association increases the overall length of the course, narrows the fairway, and makes the rough and green difficult. Thereby everyone had to keep their hands busy with all sorts of these things.

Tiger in fact brought about a period of change in all tools used in golf, including improved driver performance and corresponding ball changes through more scientific and detailed analysis and competition between companies.

Tiger showed that 'long shots' are the best weapon in golf, but in reality, driver shots were a weakness that he could not hide his anxiety throughout his career. After a knee injury and changing his swing style after meeting with new coach Hank Haney, his driver became more unstable, and there were many times when he showed unstable performances because of his driver.

"If the driver is going straight, it is difficult for anyone to control it." And he himself said, "If my family name had been Fairway instead of Woods, I would have performed much better." Did he make a self-depreciating joke?

On the other hand, the iron shot was very

good. Especially long irons that he doesn't like to use these days, like number 2 or 3-iron, he often used those irons that are replaced by hybrid or low wood numbers these days, and through this, he compensated for the weakness of the driver, which had unstable direction.

Tiger, who started playing golf on the green and around the green under the guidance of his father, was instinctively good at chip shots and putts, and was also good at short games, with some critics saying, "The essence of Tiger's golf is played on the green and around the green." It was very outstanding. People often refer to Phil Mickelson as the 'short game master, but he only made a lot of impact with creative and challenging shots, and yet it was Tiger who often played a short game that was safe and led to actual wins.

In his prime time, the stability of his putts was also very good. As his father, Earl Woods, taught him, he drew the lie of the green he was seeing in his head and putted as he saw it, and this method was always effective in urgent moments. In fact, when a survey was conducted by tour colleagues about the "skill they most want to take away from their competitors," Tiger's putting was ranked first.

As a player with excellent overall swing skills,

he divided all shots into high and low and freely hit draw and fade shots. He did not hesitate to try these techniques in major tournaments where tension was high, and succeeded, leaving an impactful impression on golf fans. and left behind numerous highlight films.

His mentality was also very good, and he seemed like he was going to eat his opponent, and he barely showed a smile during the game and showed his coolness by not even dealing with the gallery. Due to the high level of concentration and competitive spirit shown during matches, he had no competitors to follow him during his prime time. He knew how to recover immediately when he made a mistake, and he also had the ability to manage the game astutely, knowing how to get the gallery's support for his own through the 'uppercut' ceremony.

Even a professional said it was a great shot. Jim Furik, a major winner and one of the top 10 prize money winners of all time, said, "I had a chance to see Tiger's shots in real life while playing a practice round at the Ryder Cup together. Well, I'm just hitting enough shots that I think I can win thanks to this guy as long as I don't make any big mistakes" He said in an interview, "Distance is not the problem, but if you see the club hit the ball and extend, you'll know what I'm talking about." Other PGA Tour colleagues also said, "Every time I see it, I'm surprised at how different the quality of the shot is." He had a different level of shot-making ability.

D. Tiger's winning process and twists and turns

Tiger's championships from 1996 to 2019 were always close to top of the victory and, in the previous 10 years, he had a record that no one could beat, but from the middle of the years, he had to face difficulties due to various incidents such as physical abnormalities and a shameful affair incident. However, in 2019, he finally recovered and won the Masters Tournament again, reviving the dignity of the golf emperor, but then suffered a serious traffic accident and injured his foot, raising doubts as to whether he would ever be able to return to the field again.

In 2000, Tiger Woods' best season of all time, he recorded a total of 26 under par in eight weekend rounds out of four major tournaments. In the late 90s to the first decades of 2000s, Tiger had a fierce momentum that other players could not even think of chasing him. He used to hold the championship trophy in his hand.

Before 2009, out of a total of 94 rounds of

major tournaments in which Tiger participated, there were 39 cases in which he recorded 70 strokes under par. It was a great record considering that it was a major tournament where one could aim for the win even with a total score of over par for four rounds. However, in the major tournaments he participated in after that, he only recorded under 70 strokes three times in 26 weekend rounds.

Until 2013, Tiger's last peak, there were still opportunities for him to win additional major championships, but in the 20 major championships since 2009, Tiger had 9 TOP 10 finishes, including 6 times of 4th. He achieved excellent results, including those listed above. but thereafter he just didn't win.

Tiger's 15th major championship seemed a long way off due to his poor performance in the final round because of continued injuries and subsequent decline in stamina. It is true that even in 2018, when he successfully returned from injury, his chances of winning seemed low because he did not show the same charisma as in the past in the 3rd and 4th rounds of major competitions where he was in the championship bracket.

However, In the 2019 Masters Tournament, he entered the final round two strokes behind the leader, and won with a record of 2 under par in the fourth round following 5 under par in the third round, achieving the great feat of 'comeback victory in a major tournament' for the first time in his career. He achieved it. It was a valuable victory that erased his long slump in the 3rd and 4th rounds, showing his health to golf fans around the world.

By 2008, Tiger had won a total of 14 major championships and was the only player to win all of them. However, after being dealt an unexpected blow to Yang Yong-eun at the 2009 PGA Championship, the tremendous charisma and performance he showed in his 14 wins was not felt. So, he changed swing coaches four times, but the results were not satisfactory. The only notable results were Tiger's injury and Major's continued failure.

Tiger's knee, which had been broken since his college days, was a 'fatal injury' to the existing coach, and he continued to study swings that utilized Tiger's natural body type and worked hard to win, but in the face of constantly passing time, the knee kept breaking down. Due to his body, Tiger was left wondering whether he would be able to continue his career as a player with less confidence than before.

As of 2017, it was difficult for Tiger, who did

not trust his swing, not even receive physical help he could rely on mentally, to have any hope that he would be able to win 15 major games.

Jack Nicklaus won his last major, the Masters Tournament, in 1986 at the age of 46. However, Jack never suffered a fatal injury during his career, and at the time it was not a tour environment where younger players were prevalent as of now.

For Tiger, who was in his mid−40s and suffered from a serious injury that made everyday life uncomfortable, this Masters tournament was his 15th major. Hoping for a miracle called 'winning' sounded like a pretty unreasonable request. And yet In 2017, he changed direction by not having a swing coach and increasing the proportion of training to minimize body injuries.

Thus, 2018, in which many injuries were corrected, ended as a year in which an answer to the 'unreasonable demand' of achieving a 15th major was expected. He showed enough performance to raise expectations that he might achieve his 15th major victory. And at the Masters Tournament held in April 2019, he won his 5th Masters championship, his first major championship in 11 years. It was his 15th career major win.

3. Recent trends in the golf world

A. Spread of golf boom and increase of golf participation

When the 2nd World War ended in 1945, all of the colonies were liberated and new nations were born, and each liberated nation freely established its own nation, calling for freedom and independence.

However, since most of these countries were under the influence of the British Empire, even if they were liberated, they could not immediately escape British influence, and on the contrary, they accepted some parts of British culture and continued it, thereby preserving and cultivating British culture.

As golf, one of the accepted cultures, spread throughout each country, and golf culture expanded globally. As golf courses increased in each country and the number of people playing golf increased, golf which started in Scotland in northern England, has expanded worldwide today.

Meanwhile, as the United States of America developed into an independent country at the end of the 18th century, it virtually inherited Britain's golf culture and built and operated numerous golf courses on its vast land, rivaling Britain and becoming the de facto center of world golf culture today.

Therefore, today the center of golf is divided into the United Kingdom and the United States, but in reality, the power of the United States has grown, and half of the world's golf courses are in the United States. Furthermore, the center of all golf culture has moved to the United States, forming the majority of important golf tournaments and activities to be held there. So It can be said that now most of the golf activities is taking place in the United States. There are 38,081 golf courses in the world, and courses distributed by country around the world is shown as in the tables below, and there are about 500 courses under construction or planned, with about half of the increase being concentrated in the United States, followed by Japan, the United Kingdom, Canada, and Australia. However, Japan's golf courses are different from those in the other four countries due to their short distance and small size.

According to the current announcement from Britain's R&A, the number of golfers in the United States is 39.6 million, 34% increase from 7 years ago.

The Royal Golf Association (R&A) handed over its report in February 2024, excluding the United States. There is a confident field golf population in 2016 of 29.6 million but it increased to 34.5 million in 2020.

Following the increase in number, the number increased again by 15% in two years. A total of 61.2 million people are said to participate in golf, including great par 3 golf on agreeable courses, indoor individual (simulator) golf and use of the personal range. "The popularity of golf has soared in recent years, both on courses and in alternative formats," explains Phil Anderson, R&A's chief development officer.

It is important to note that the golf population has increased even after the pandemic, and among them, the population of alternative courses such as screen golf has increased. Mr Anderson added: "We need to encourage more people to get involved in sport."

According to the R&A's February 2024 report, Asia had a notable growth in golf-related population and market among R&A jurisdictions, with 22.5 million golf participants in Asia, followed by Europe with 21.1 million. Even when limited to the field golf population alone, Asia had the largest population at 16.1 million, and Europe was second with 14 million.

Looking at the golf population by country, Japan had the largest population at 8.1 million, followed by Canada (5.6 million), South Korea (5.35 million), the United Kingdom (3.4 million), and Germany (2.1 million). If we include the United States, which has the largest golfing population, Korea ranks fourth in the world.

If we look only at Korea, we can see the rapid growth of golf recently. In Korea,

Starting this year, the Korea Golf Association(KGA), with Naver and Smart Score, are carrying out a handicap promotion campaign, but the number of registered golfers is only a portion of the actual golf population, and the golf population in Korea is calculated to be 5.35 million, and the total number of courses, from 18 holes to 9 holes and par 3 courses, was reported to be 844 and the number of golfers per course was 6,339.

Meanwhile, when combined with the U.S. golf population data report released last year by the National Golf Foundation (NGF), a picture of the entire global village is drawn. NGF estimates that the number of people over the age of six who enjoy golf in the U.S. totals 37.5 million, a 17% increase compared to five years ago.

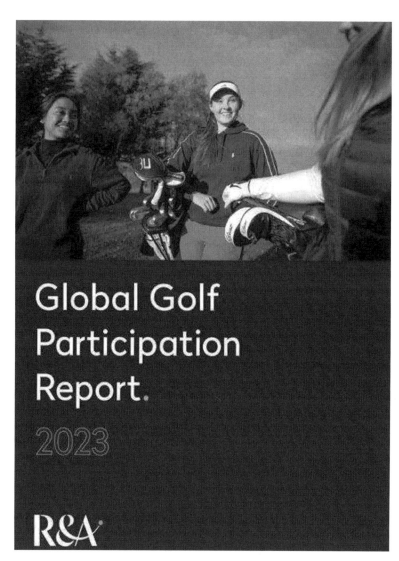

Global Golf
Participation
Report.
2023

R&A

R&A Report in February of 2024

3. Recent trends

According to the NGF of the United States, the number of people in the United States who enjoyed playing only on the golf course was 12.6 million, the number of people who only enjoyed Top golf, Drive Sack, Screen Golf, and Driving Range outside the golf course was 12.4 million, and the number of people who enjoyed playing both inside and outside the course was 12.5 million.

If you combine the entire global data from the R&A and NGF, the total number of people using golf courses is 64.7 million, but if you include the population participating in golf such as simulation, Topgolf, and driving range users, there are 98.7 million people playing golf among the 8 billion people in the world.

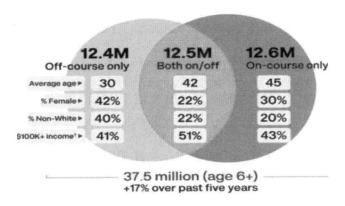

	12.4M Off-course only	12.5M Both on/off	12.6M On-course only
Average age ►	30	42	45
% Female ►	42%	22%	30%
% Non-White ►	40%	22%	20%
$100K+ income† ►	41%	51%	43%

37.5 million (age 6+)
+17% over past five years

NGF report on golf population of USA

Meanwhile, statistics on the golf population active at such golf courses vary depending on the organization that produces the statistics, so it is not completely reliable, but I think the trend can be estimated to some extent. Looking back at Korea's recent statistical indicators, according to the '2021 Korean Golf Index', the number of people active in golf in 2021 was estimated at 11.76 million, or 31.5% of the total population, an increase of 16.4% from 2017. Among the detailed types, the 'continuous golf active population (23.2%)' was analyzed to be about 8.65 million people, and the 'new golf active population (8.3%)' was analyzed to be about 3.11 million people.

World golf fields by continent

continents	courses	%	fields
North America	19,826	(51%,	17,298)
Europe	8,940	(23%,	7,132)
Asia	6,349	(17%,	4,517)
Oceania	2,109	(5%,	1,998)
Africa	932	(2%,	875)
South America	708	(2%,	651)
	38,864	100%	27,471

B. Increase in golf prize money

As the golf boom began, players from around the world began to flock to competitions in the US and UK, and by winning there, they made a huge amount of money.

At the beginning of the century, when Tiger swept four major championships, a new word was coined, Tiger Slam, and he went from a prodigy to a so-called emperor of golf by winning a lot of money.

While he was suffering from a driving accident, the Spanish JON Rahm stood out. Now he has won the prize money.

The amount of prize money they receive has increased every year, and now, with just one win in a major tournament, the prize money is worth millions of dollars, or billions of won in Korean currency, so it is no exaggeration to say that the game of golf has become a golden game.

When I see a young Korean player named Seongjae Lim playing with them, I can't help but feel my heart swell.

A new word, Tiger Slam, was even coined to

refer to Tiger Woods winning Major tournaments at British, U.S. and PGA Championships in the year 2000 and then the Masters Tournament in 2001.

In golf, winning all four major tournaments in a year is called a Grand Slam, and winning all major tournaments in a career is called a Career Grand Slam. Tiger Woods won the 2000 British Open and U.S Open. At the same time, he achieved the Career Grand Slam and the so-called Tiger Slam by winning the PGA Championship that year and the Masters Tournament in 2001.

Jon Rham, who won the Masters in 2023, broke the PGA season's highest prize money. Jon Rahm (Spain) won the Masters Tournament, the first major of the PGA Tour, known as the 'Festival of Masters,' and broke the all-time season's highest prize money by adding $3.24 million (KRW 4,273 million won) in prize money.

Jon Rahm won the 87th Masters held at Augusta National Golf Club (par 72, 7,475 yards) in Augusta, USA, earning his 4th win of the season and rising to $13,288,540 (KRW 17.53 billion) in prize money, surpassing previous leader Scotty Scheffler (USA). The world golf ranking also rose from 3rd to 1st.

Jon Rahm broke the season's highest prize

money by winning the Masters. Jon Rahm (Spain) won the first major masters tournament on the PGA Tour, known as the 'Festival of Masters,' and broke the all-time season's highest prize money by adding $3.24 million (4.273 billion won) in prize money.

Rahm, who won $2.7 million by winning the Sentry Tournament held in Hawaii earlier that year, earned $1.368 million by winning the American Express and a whopping $3.6 million by winning the Genesis Invitational. The year's 13 PGA Tour special tournaments have a total prize money of $20 million, and he won two of them, and by winning the Masters, he broke the previous season's total prize money.

The PGA Tour's all-time leader in prize money for a single season is Scotty Scheffler(USA), who won four times, including the Masters the year before, with $13,176,910 in the 2021-22 season. Schaeffler maintained the lead with $11,631,495 until the last week. This is because he won The Players, which had the highest prize money (a total of $25 million), and the WM Phoenix Open, a special tournament.

As he tied for 10th place in this Masters and received $432,000, his season prize money dropped to second place ($12,063,495) after Rahm. However, it is almost twice as much as third place Max Homa (USA)'s $7.77 million.

Schaeffler's winnings alone so far have moved him up to third place on the season. With nearly half of the season still remaining, it is unusual for the two players' prize money to surpass previous season prize money records.

Looking at the total season prize money record, Vijay Singh (Fiji), who won 9 times in one season, including the 2004 Major PGA Championship, ranked 5th ($10.9 million). Tiger Woods (USA) ranked 6th in the 2006~2007 season, in which he won 7 times in addition to the Major PGA Championship, and was in the top 10 four times.

Players who were top prize money winners in previous seasons usually won the Masters or PGA Championship that year. This was the case with Rahm and Scheffler, Jordan Spieth and Woods in the past years.

2023's total prize money, announced by Augusta National, is $18 million (23.742 billion won), an increase of $3 million from the previous year's $15 million. The winning prize money also increased by $540,000 from $2.7 million the year before.

4. Dream of Albatross

An albatross, a giant bird of the sky that flies 90,000 miles. It is a distance that is so fascinating and majestic that everyone wants to fly over it at least once. It has been people's dream and hope since ancient times. As a result, numerous means and methods were studied and developed, and so many tools were invented. However, humans themselves cannot fly. Even if you jump high with a pole, you are still just the main character of the earth. So the albatross may be an eternal dream.

But dreams do come true. People have been working tirelessly to make this dream come true. The dream of making the ball fly farther led to the Deca Driver, which was made with new materials and a new shape, and eventually developed into the Super Driver.

Meanwhile, the wish to swing the ball high in the sky leads to various swings, making the dreams of birdies, eagles, and albatross come true.

A. Distance and accuracy in golf

Golf is ultimately a game of distance and accuracy. In order to conquer a certain distance from the teeing area(ground) to the green, you must first approach the target by hitting a long distance. And when approaching the target point, it is not always necessary to attack it from a long distance, but it is possible to attack it from a short distance, so it is necessary to balance long and short distances.

Conquering these distances inevitably requires accuracy of shots.

You must drop it exactly at the target point, otherwise you may end up going OB (out of bounds), entering the water, or getting stuck in the rough and having a hard time getting out.

Moreover, when you get close to the target, you must secure the correct distance with an accurate shot to get over the bunker surrounding the green and land the ball on the green, or you will most likely end up in a bunker and be in trouble.

Also, if you fall into the rough around the green, even if it is not necessarily a bunker, you have to approach the hole, sometimes by pitching or sometimes with a lob shot, to get out of there.

In these cases, sense and sense are sometimes required rather than strength. Even when you stand on the putting green, if you do not have a thorough sense of distance, direction measurement, and the ability to point out the green surface, you may miss your goal two or three times even when your target hole are right in front of your eyes.

Furthermore, even if you are able to maintain a certain degree of distance and accuracy, if it rains or is sometimes windy and your senses and vision become blurred, everything becomes disorganized in an instant.

This is because golf is a sport played by people, so one's physical strength and senses are absolutely necessary,

and since these conditions are greatly influenced by natural and physiological changes, the problem is that a single movement cannot be performed uniformly.

Golf is something that seems surprisingly simple, but becomes more difficult and interesting the more you dig into it.

Meanwhile, as a tool to conquer distance and

achieve accuracy, we use 14 clubs. In other words, it can be said to be equivalent to a weapon.

The utility of a weapon varies greatly depending on the abilities of the person using it. Sometimes there are people who are good at long distances, and sometimes there are people who are good at securing accuracy, and those who have both are more likely to win. In that sense, golf can be said to be a sport of harmony and balance.

B. Driver and driving distance

How many people cried and laughed at their tee shot? The strategy for every hole begins with a tee shot at the teeing area (or ground), and the success of the first stroke determines whether or not the hole can be mastered.

Therefore, in order to hit the first stroke well, regardless of whether you are a professional or an amateur, you try to send the ball to a safe spot on the fairway by holding the driver and hitting it as hard as you can, that is, hitting it farther and straighter.

To achieve this, we spend countless hours practicing driver swings and prepare for this by purchasing new drivers or developing new hitting methods.

A driver is ultimately a weapon that produces distance. Distance is only possible when the ball flies high in the sky and has a long flight time, but once it hits the ground, it has a lot of runs and rolls endlessly. These long-hit requirements depend on the angle of the ball, the initial speed of the ball, and the rotation of the ball.

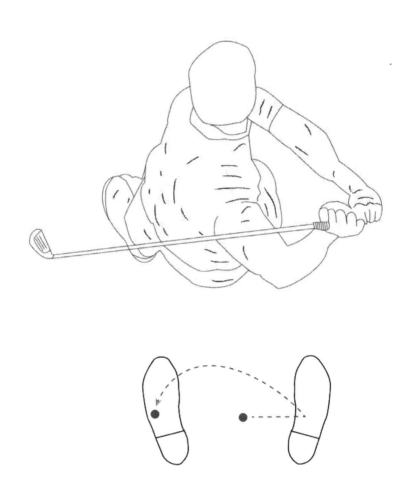

The loft of the club head determines the angle at which the ball flies. In the case of drivers, the loft is usually between 9 and 12 degrees. Powerful professionals hit long shots over 270 to over 300 yards with a 9 degree big driver and aim for an eagle or birdie by using a short iron for middle holes and a middle or long iron for long holes.

To accelerate the initial speed of the ball, the circular motion must be increased to accelerate the speed of the club head. So the length of the shaft became longer. Recently, clubs over 45 inches have been released.

While the amateur's ball rises high in the sky from the beginning and then falls, the professional's ball flies as a fastball and then gradually flies in a parabolic curve. Recently, I am curious to see how far the driver's horsepower will go as there is research being done on hitting methods that accelerate the run.

A recent feature of creating drivers that produce such distances was first the creation of large club heads. As the head grows, the sweet spot naturally widens, making it easier to hit the ball.

In the past, if a club head was made larger, it became heavier and difficult to control, so it was not made large. However, with the development of science, new materials were developed, from persimmon to metal, and from metal to titanium, making it ultra—light and strengthening its strength.

In addition, as the weight of the club shaft became lighter, a driver with a shaft length that was 1 or 2 inches longer than before was created.

Would it be said that golf clubs have now entered the era of competition? There have been rapid changes in the golf club market.

Until recently, American Callaway golf clubs were popular among metal woods, but these days, Hiro Honma metal wood drivers have become popular and are receiving one, two, three, four stars.

Also, the fact that people are lining up to buy various drivers said to be made of titanium, even though they are rare items that cannot be purchased for money, shows the development of technology and science to satisfy golfers' desire to achieve sky—high distances.

It goes without saying that when you hit the first stroke long enough to land on the fairway with such a driver, you can easily make the second and third fairway shots or approach shots.

Driver shot is the first step in golf.

Nevertheless, the further you fly, the more severe the directional bias due to small errors, sometimes resulting in a slice, sometimes a hook, and the ball does not fall on the fairway but goes OB or goes into the rough, resulting in disappointment.

It is said that even in the case of PGA pros, the fairway hit rate stays in the 70–80% range, so you can guess what it is like for amateur golfers.

Most amateur golfers use clubs that have very low lofts and long shafts that are not only difficult to control but also do not fit well, so it is not easy to use a driver well.

However, those who overcome this will win, and those who cannot overcome it will collapse. Therefore, theories and secrets to conquering drivers have been constantly evolving.

C. Moment of impact
and swing plane theory

Address and swing are ultimately the basic movements to achieve the moment when the club head hits the ball. However, no matter how weak a woman's swing is, it is difficult to see the moment of impact with our eyes and we can only judge it by looking at the direction and distance of the ball hit, so we must make a good decision based on numerous practices and theories. Isn't it true that you hit several boxes of balls a day to make an impact?

Of course, a good swing creates a good impact, but sometimes the ball rolls to the ground or becomes a mid-air ball without you realizing it, and sometimes you get hooked and sliced repeatedly, which is often embarrassing.

No matter how much expert you are, if you feel unwell in the early morning or tired in the afternoon, you may have experienced that the ball flies in the wrong direction and you know you hit it incorrectly.

Therefore, swing theories to eliminate these miss shots and hit the ball straight have been continuously developed, and the famous one among them is the swing plane theory.

Simply put, the swing plane is the same virtual plane where the club head is consistently moved through the back swing, down swing, and follow-through and finish after impact. It means the ball running the ideal flat surface.

Only then can the club head hit the ball straight toward the target by maintaining a constant circular motion of the club head centered on the spine.

However, unlike this accurate swing, in reality, at the moment of hitting the ball, there are inside-to-out, outside-to-in, and inside-to-in based on the club head. You can assume three directions, and each throws a hook ball, slice ball, and strong fastball.

Due to the shape of the ball, the part that hits the round ball will definitely be a point on one side. However, even if it is only one point, the hit area is not just the center right side, but can be several points up and down depending on the angle of the loft, so the direction of the ball is bound to change depending on the result of hitting.

Considering the circular motion of the swing and the fact that the ball is round, the moment of impact is clearly only a single moment, but the result appears different due to the action of this single moment, so it can be said this is the end point of the golf swing practiced throughout a lifetime.

To help you understand, if we look at the example of playing billiards, we sometimes hit a point in the center of the ball, but we also hit a point on the top and bottom or on the left and right, creating infinite harmony of billiard balls.

Even though there is a difference in size of the ball and the cue, the movement of the ball can be said to vary greatly depending on the strength and direction of the force acting on it. Therefore, in order to control the force applied to the ball, we created 14 clubs, each with a different loft to control the area where it hits, so you can achieve the desired results by using the 14 weapons appropriately at each time. This can be said to be golf, but the result appears different due to the action of this single moment, so it can be said this is the end point of the golf swing practiced throughout a lifetime.

Not only do most amateurs not have the luxury of choosing the hardness of the ball, but they often use the ball they received as a prize for winning or participating in a friendly golf tournament or a ball bought by a friend.

However, when you go to a game, wouldn't your score be good if you chose the ball that suits you and hit it?

At the very least, if the moment of impact is a continuous movement, even if small, it is necessary to hit a ball with a hardness that suits you and stabilize the direction of the ball by keeping the swing trajectory constant.

D. Upper blow and down blow

When you watch a PGA Tour pro's iron shot, you can see on TV that he hits the ball while throwing a fist-sized lump of dirt. Almost all of their iron shots are made with a down blow, hitting the ball before the club head passes the lowest point, resulting in a powerful shot like this, but on a tee shot, it is down blow shot or an upper blow shot.

Opinions are divided as to whether this is the case. In general, even in textbooks, it is said to hit a driver shot with the ball on the left foot side, so there is a question as to whether the club head should be hit after passing the lowest point, so some people hold the driver and hit an upper blow shot.

The problem at this time is that, in the case of address, the grip is generally held in a Y-shape or inverted K-shape and the V-shape direction is told to aim at the right shoulder, so the right palm gradually falls under the club and looks toward the sky, moving towards the left target. and you keep deviating from the basic posture of being at a right angle.

In addition, with this grip, the right armpit opens during the back swing, which disrupts the direction of the swing and makes the direction of the ball unstable, making it impossible to hit the ball with ease, so the distance is shorter than expected.

In order to prevent this kind of evil from experience, we need to recall the time when we were children and stood by the river and threw stones with all our might. At this time, we remember that if we pull our elbows back without opening them wide from our armpits and throw them, the stone will fly far away.

I think that the shortcut to a smooth swing is to extend your left hand during the backswing and turn it back while thinking about the form of slinging your right hand. This is because as long as the ball's direction goes straight, you can hit long shots with confidence. At this time, you have more distance and can choose your target point at will, which allows you to think strategically and significantly reduce your score.

After that, all you have to do is to shoot regardless of whether it is an upper blow or a down blow. Therefore, when practicing at the practice range, you should pay more attention to placing the ball in the best position and maintaining body balance by adjusting the rhythm and tempo.

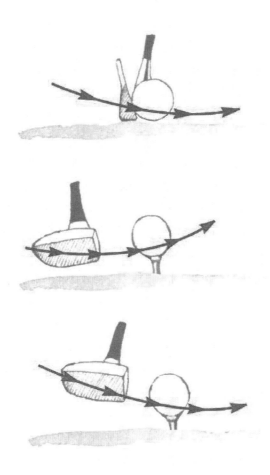

5. Universal gravitation and swing plane theory

Isaac Newton discovered the universal law of gravitation when he saw an apple fall from a tree. In other words, all objects in the universe have mutual attraction, and the law of universal gravitation acts depending on distance and mass. It is deeply mysterious to think that this law is also applied to golf.

Since a golf ball has the same mass as an apple, would it be able to withstand this enormous universal gravitational pull from the center of the Earth? So, no matter how hard we hit the golf ball, it will fall down within 300 yards at most, so it can be said that there are not many people who do not know this law and try to hit it more than 400 yards. We thought we were just going out to have fun and played a lot of golf ball, but aren't we just playing in the palm of God's hand? That is the law of universal gravitation and a golf ball? Have you ever think about it ever? Wouldn't it be fun to think about universal gravitation while playing golf?

A. Basic golf posture and
swing movement

The basic movement of golf is believed to be swing. In order to fix the four limbs, hold the golf club and hit the ball at the desired distance it is most important to take the basic posture, enter the motion of hitting the ball, that is, swing, and hit the ball in the target direction.

However, since each person's body is different from the birth and performs various tasks during the growing process, each person's body is different, so it can be said that each person's swing motion is also different. To give a simple example, a right-handed person can easily sharpen a pencil with his right hand, but it is difficult to sharpen it with his left hand because he has mainly used his right hand while growing up.

However, just as it is difficult for a left-hander to sharpen a pencil with his right hand, and just as we change depending on how we were raised during the process of growing up, everyone develops certain habits as they grow up, and this results in different golf swings. So It is usually not easy to predict results.

Depending on how you swing, you can get a variety of results, so to overcome this, you must constantly learn and train swing movements. In that sense, it can be said that golf skills must be learned from an early age and must be practiced continuously to develop the habit. so It is not only difficult to change them, but it becomes more and more fixed and difficult to change.

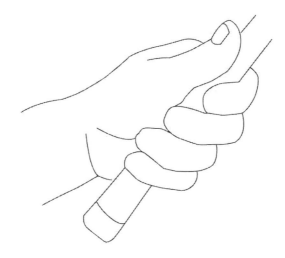

However, even as golf spread throughout the world after 2nd World War, there was no significant change in the advancement of golf because it was considered a kind of upper-class gentleman's game and was difficult for common people to play unless people had a secured social status and a certain amount of money.

However, it can be said that a major tectonic shift occurred as not only did each country achieve economic recovery and create more leisure times after the war, and the center of golf moved from Europe to the American continent.

In particular, golf, which boasted that it was a white person's game and looked down on black people, developed rapidly toward the end of the 20th century as it became open to all races, especially black people.

There were some black pioneers who made efforts in this direction, but around the end of the 20th century, the emergence of 'Tiger Woods' who had an early interest in this field and grew up under his father's training and guidance, and his performance was almost ground breaking in golf. It would be fair to say that these kind of changes around the world of golf played an almost decisive role.

At first, no one would have known that the power of one individual would be so great. However, it can be said that not only was the power of his father, who discovered Tiger Woods' talent in this direction earlier than anyone else and supported him, absolutely great, but also the support of Nike, which supported him from early, was also great.

Tiger Woods' achievements, which changed the world of golf since 1997, did not stop until 2010, and it is no exaggeration to say that there is no one who does not know this kind of golf world as the size of golf tournaments has skyrocketed and the prize money has also increased massively.

Even after his father passed away and he was caught up in an love affair and took a temporary break, his desire for golf never ceased. Nobody deny that Tiger Woods' achievements changed the world of golf since 1997.

It is no exaggeration to say that modern golf is changing from the very beginning. As the conventional, old-fashioned gentlemanly game suddenly grew into a popular sport worldwide, the number of people who loved golf increased rapidly, and golf courses to accommodate them were built all over the world.

B. Golf grip and swing movement

There are many types of golf swings, but in order to swing while holding a golf club, the most important thing is how to hold the golf club, that is, the grip.

However, there are many types of golf clubs, from drivers to putters, and the grip can vary depending on whether you hit it long or short, and furthermore, it can be different depending on which direction you hit the ball, so you should take lessons from an instructor at first. This is advantageous.

It is common sense to hold the golf club in the most comfortable position and hit the ball comfortably, but there are different grips for each person, and these days, it is said that it is better to hold the golf club with a normal grip.

C. Exercise of Golf Swing

The basics of golf are swings. Golf swing, which involves holding a golf club and striking a golf ball in the desired direction and at a desired distance, is an exercise that cannot be performed well without practice.

These swings are different depending on the person, and even the same person can produce wildly different swings depending on morning and evening, summer and winter, and various locations, and the results are different.

We see tall people and short people, fat people and slim people, adults and children, men and women, and their gaits are all very different from person to person. You can see it.

In other words, the reason why the gait of ordinary people is so different is because each person walks differently as they grow up and become a habit that has become ingrained in their body. Moreover, it is natural that even beginners who are just starting to learn with a golf club have different swings. This means that, conversely, it is impossible to get the ball to the target without constantly practicing the golf swing.

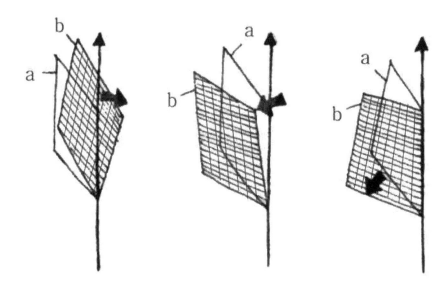

Now that golf has become popular and everyone can play golf, when different people play golf in a group, the results are wildly different and many unintentional mistakes are made.

Conversely, this means that golf requires constant practice and a certain level of confidence, and even more so, anyone who wants to become a golfer must practice more than anyone else and aim to win, and the road is difficult. It can't be helped.

In that sense, I believe that in golf, you have to practice constantly and play better than anyone else to win and even receive more prize money.

This fact applies not only to golf players, but also to general golfers, such as amateur golfers or social golfers. In that regard, as the golfing population increases, the number of golf driving ranges has increased, and a variety of driving ranges have been created, which is why many people who want to play golf are coming and going here.

Therefore, do not think about playing golf without practice. If you have decided to play golf, the first duty of a golfer is to run to the driving range whenever you have time and practice very often times. Tiger, the world's golfing genius, also has a golf driving range in a large space at his home, and he practices golf whenever he has time. Furthermore, his young child, Charles, can practice anytime right at home, making him an excellent golfer at such a young age. Then you are improving your grades.

In that sense, golf must start with practice, and golf skills that do not practice will not improve. Now, let's start by looking for a golf driving range next to the house.

6. Machiavelli's Wisdom

People constantly fight over and over again. A fight must be won. So, all kinds of tricks and secrets are developed and new weapons are developed to lead the war to victory. Human wisdom also develops, and new civilizations begin from this. Therefore, theories for winning wars were developed early on, with Sun Tzu in the East and Machiavelli in the West.

Golf is also a game that needs to be won. So, all sorts of wisdom is mobilized to win the game. Stand at the teeing area, examine the terrain ahead, choose the path to attack, and grab the club. Sometimes straight, sometimes left and sometimes right, we run down an unknown path with the ball in front of us while holding the club firm.

A. Standing on the teeing area

One of the characteristics of Korean golf courses is that a separate rubber mat or artificial grass is laid on the teeing area, and tee shots are forced there.

Due to the difficulty of lawn care by seasonal changes of spring, summer, autumn and winter, in the name of protecting the lawn, lines are put up there and people are not allowed to enter the grass on the teeing area and are told to hit only on the mat.

Can amateur golfers dream of teeing off on silky grass? To be honest, the teeing area grass, which is completely closed to visitors except for club championship tournaments or international tournaments that may or may not be held once a year, is to be decreasing more than half the interest in golf.

When an amateur golfer stands on the mat and tries to take an address position, the spikes get caught between the rubber bands, making it impossible to take a proper stance. The mat is usually twisted in one direction, which can cause a miss shot for average golfers who otherwise have difficulty orienting themselves.

In addition, the front part of the teeing area which is supposed to be flat, usually sits down, causing golfers who do not hit the ball to make a mistake with a ground ball shot from the first hole.

Regardless of the direction of the mat, even if you aim and address the target point on the fairway, people's optical illusions are unavoidable, so pulling or pushing the club at the moment of swing often causes the ball to miss, which can be truly embarrassing from the first hit. This is the teeing area situation at a Korean golf course.

Of course, this doesn't happen when you go abroad. By regularly moving the tee—marker and managing the grass, tee shots are allowed on green grass, giving golfers a fresh taste and allowing them to enjoy the delicacy of a great shot. The problem is how to realistically overcome tee shots on Korean—style mats.

You should never overdo the tee shot when your posture is bad. If the tee shot is hit well, the ball will fall far into the fairway target, but if it is hit wrong, the miss is worse than any other shot.

In other words, most average golfers suffer from more slices, which is a chronic problem, and advanced golfers often have severe hooks, causing the ball to fall in a position where it is very difficult to hit the next shot.

To prevent these mistakes, you must first set up by selecting a flat area suitable for maximum swing within the given teeing area.

Vaguely hitting the ball in the exact same spot as the person in front of you or addressing it without knowing the direction properly can lead to a missed shot. The shortcut to preventing missed shots is to choose the best spot on the mat and shoot with a controlled swing without being overly ambitious.

B. The importance of setup

When an amateur golfer stands on the mat and tries to take an address position, the spikes get caught between the rubber bands, making it impossible to take a proper stance. The mat is usually twisted in one direction, which can cause a miss shot for average golfers who otherwise have difficulty orienting themselves.

Like in Korea, when a rubber mat is laid out on the teeing area and a tee marker is inserted into it, the direction in which the tee mat is placed is often not exactly aligned with the direction in which the player should actually hit, and even if a mat is not laid, Gwanak course is not played directly. There are some teeing areas that face to the right, like the first hole of CC's West Course.

In places like this, even if you recognize it and set up both feet to take an address stance, you cannot determine the target point, so the ball often flies toward the right and lands in the OB area. In particular, high handicappers, who hit in the 90s or higher, usually fall into temptation and make wrong mistakes from the beginning, which ruins their mood and greatly affects their score.

Most players who hit the driver not straight and are not clearly aware of the landing point of the ball make this mistake. In order to avoid making this mistake, we must pay special attention to the setup posture, which is easy to think about when getting on the ground.

In these cases, pros usually stand behind the teeing area and decide on the target direction. Take a picture of an immediately visible target, such as a large pine tree in the distance, the left side of a bunker, or a turret in an apartment, then set up both feet and enter the address posture.

This case is not simple either. The plane of the ground is tilted because one part is high, or the front part is relatively lower than the back part, so the ball does not float well, and there are times when the ball does not float well, and because of the marks left by the person in front of you, you have to put both feet on the ground tightly and address the ball. There are so many times when your posture is unstable.

Therefore, although tee shots are allowed

within a fairly wide range in accordance with Article 11 of the Golf Rules, which allows tee shots from any location within two club lengths back from the two tee markers, in most cases, a tee shot is hit from the spot where the person in front hit it.

However, since most tee shots need to be hit to a good place for the second hit, you need to check whether you hit where you intended rather than smiling simply because you hit it far.

It is said that amateur golfers initially hit a slice ball, then gradually move on to a hook ball and then hit it straight, but it is customary for the ball to go in a straight line and tilt to either the left or right as soon as it falls. Therefore, some people recommend hitting the fade ball from the right marker and the draw ball from the left marker.

Doing so allows you to utilize a much wider target space than aiming at the middle of the fairway, which is effective in preventing missed shots.

Considering various circumstances, it can be said that the teeing area gives players a wide range of options and gives them the opportunity to address with the best setup in the best position. There is a need to exercise that right.

C. Conquer the world
with your grip

A grip that holds the club. The importance of the grip, which acts as a connection through which the entire body's movements are transmitted to the club, is described in detail in golf techniques, but nothing is as neglected as the grip during practice or in actual play.

Swing form and body movements are noticeable during the stroke, so the instructor or the person next to you can comment on them, but the grip is often overlooked because it is hidden in the momentary movement.

However, no matter how strong you are and how good your body movements are, the results will vary depending on your grip, so as you become more advanced, you will learn techniques to adjust your grip and fly the ball in the desired direction.

Strangely, depending on the person, both hands are not the same length, and some people may have relatively long left or right hands.

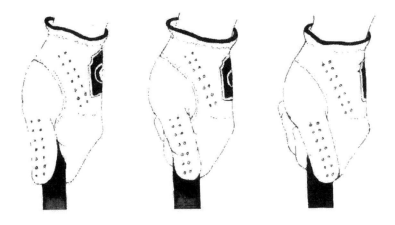

Therefore, there are people who have to use the ten finger grip, or baseball grip, rather than the widely popular overlapping grip, or vardon grip, and the interlocking grip. Some people supplement their strength with an interlocking grip.

Also, young people who first start playing golf usually do not know the exact cause of a slice, so they try changing from a palm grip to a finger grip, or from a square grip to a strong grip. Even if you change it, the slice is not corrected and sometimes gets worse.

Because it is important to choose a grip that suits your physique and hold it comfortably, overlapping can not necessarily be forced, or even if you use overlapping, slices, hooks, and distances are not all resolved.

The problem is that the grip acts like a fitting that reflects the body's swing motion onto the club, so the accuracy and balance of the swing motion must be guaranteed. However, without the correct grip, the balance of the swing movement is not guaranteed. The relationship between swing and grip is complementary.

Generally, when amateur golfers switch to a strong grip to correct a slice, they are too conscious of the teaching that the right thumb and forefinger should point to the right shoulder (V-shaped grip), so the right hand gradually bends downward, and in extreme cases, there are quite a few cases where the palm is facing the sky.

In such a case, no matter how much you want to have a good swing, not only will it not be a good swing, but if it hardens into a form, it will be very difficult to correct it later. And as you become more advanced, you will gradually learn how to use the intentional hook or intentional slice, and how to freely use the draw ball or fade ball, it is almost impossible to do it with such a grip

Therefore, amateur golfers return to the square grip through several trials and errors. In fact, only by practicing alternately between strong grip and weak grip at the practice range can you use the square grip with ease.

Also, in practice, it is sometimes unreasonable to force only one type of grip form, given that various shots are assumed, such as shots from slopes that are not necessarily flat surfaces, and tee shots, as well as wood or iron shots from the fairway. When you have to deal with various situations such as approach shots aimed at the on-green, bunker shots, and rough shots, it is unreasonable to use only a single grip.

Therefore, by trying various grips, you will need to find the grip that suits you, and constantly check and correct it so that you can control the club with that grip and achieve good scores.

When a champion was asked the secret to winning a major championship, he pointed to his left thumb and said that he benefited from using fades and draw balls freely, which clearly shows how important the grip is.

He conquered the world with his grip.

D. High tee or low tee

When hitting a tee shot, some people place the tee particularly high and hit it, while others hit it low. I don't know much at first, but as the years go by, I become more interested in the height of the tee, and tried it by putting it high or low.

Of course, it is not unknown in principle that it is recommended to place the tee so that the ball is in the middle of the club head so that it just meets the driver's sweet spot as in the textbook, but in reality, when you go out on the field, you often end up hitting ground balls. Amateurs who sometimes suffer misfortune, such as hitting an aerial ball or falling into a pond, often believe that the cause is the height of the tee and adjust the height.

We usually raise the tee for early morning golf and limit the height for daytime golf. However, hitting a ground ball or hitting an air ball is fundamentally a matter of swing hitting method, not the height of the tee.

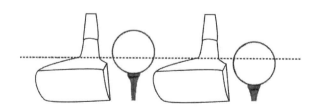

However, from experience, long hitters often set the tee high. A few years ago, I saw an American professional who came to Korea with Scott Hawk hit the tee high, swing a long ball, and hit it much farther than Scott Hawk.

The question is whether there is any change in the ball when the tee is placed high or low. It is an empirical fact that when the tee is set high, it is difficult for most amateurs to just meet the ball accurately, so the ball's flight quality is deformed and the intensity of bending left and right increases, so there is a strong tendency for it to hook or slice. In comparison, a ball on a low tee has a relatively low left–right bend, so would it be said that the probability of OB is reduced accordingly?

So, if you try to hit a long ball with the tee high in the morning when your body is not fully relaxed, the ball is likely to bend left or right, but if you hit it low, it usually becomes a ground ball and you lose distance.

Recently, with the development of technology, big head drivers, or deca–drivers, have become popular, so the tee is bound to be relatively higher. However, it can be said that the height of the tee varies depending on the striking method used. In general, people who use the down blow method and hit the ball before the club head reaches the lowest point hit it low, and conversely, people who hit the ball past the lowest point using the upper blow method usually hit it high.

In extreme cases, when making an approach shot from the fairway with an iron, the rule is to hit it with a down blow, and there is no difference in that case. Therefore, if you want to get direction, the lower the better, and if you want to give distance, it may be advantageous to place it a little higher. You will get a feel for it by practicing with different tees instead of just hitting the tee fixed to the mat at the practice range.

For amateur golfers with different swing forms, it takes a considerable amount of time to correct the swing itself, and if you are worried that you are not hitting the ball properly right away, one way would be to adjust the tee to hit the shot.

Also, when you hit your first tee shot in the early morning on Sunday before your body has even warmed up, it is easy to end up with a ground ball. In this case, you can prevent the ground ball in advance by adjusting the height of the tee. The problem is that it is an amateur golfer's privilege to adjust the height of the tee according to each person's inclination, time and place.

E. Put the first tee high

After finishing work on a Saturday afternoon, most of the golfers rushes down the highway to make it to the reservation time, and then stands at the teeing ground of the first hole without even having time to warm up. A weekend-salary golfer wakes up at 4 a. m on Sunday, runs quickly, and joins the friends at meeting plaza before the sunrise, and joins the early morning golfers who rushed to the golf course in the early morning,

And the lady golfers who came to the golf course to enjoy a long round with neighborhood friends while their husbands were at work and the children were at school. Everyone came to the field as if they were being chased by something, so that they hurry up to shot from the beginning. There's no way this could work out right.

At times like this, the next group is often waiting behind you, so it's stressful even if you don't, but the tee shot ball crawls to the ground and stops, and even if you hit it after a long time, there are times when you get a hook or slice, which can be embarrassing.

Especially when a ground ball is made and the ball lands a few meters in front of you, it is extremely embarrassing. Of course, this will be rare for golfers of a high level, but even they may have experienced this once or twice if they drive a few hours to play early morning golf.

The problem is that since golf is a sport, you have to do preliminary exercise before playing a round, but there are some cases where you cannot do that. It is customary for professionals to not only adjust their condition in advance of a match, but also come out in advance on the day of the match to warm up and practice in advance, but for amateurs to stand on the teeing ground without even doing preliminary exercises can be seen as irresponsible in some ways.

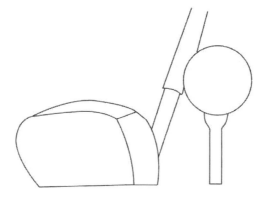

However, it is common to get out just in time, but because you can't waste time leisurely warming up, you just hit the first shot without preparation. In times like these, people have no choice but to start the round by warming up for 3 to 4 holes and adjusting their condition for the day. Therefore, it is best to take a light tee shot rather than trying to make a long hit from the beginning.

Especially when a ground ball is made and the ball lands a few meters in front of you, it is extremely embarrassing. Of course, this will be rare for golfers of a high level, but even they may have experienced this kind of shots once or twice if they drive a few hours to play early morning golf.

The problem is that since golf is a sport, you have to do preliminary exercise before playing a round, but there are some cases where you cannot do that. It is customary for professionals to not only adjust their condition in advance of a match, but also come out in advance on the day of the match to warm up and practice in advance, but for amateurs to stand on the teeing ground without even doing preliminary exercises can be seen as irresponsible in some ways.

However, it is common to get out just in time,

but because you can't waste time leisurely warming up, you just hit the first shot. In times like these, people have no choice but to start the round by warming up for 3 to 4 holes and adjusting their condition for the day. Therefore, it is best to take a light tee shot rather than trying to make a long hit from the beginning.

In a state where the body is not relaxed, there is a high probability that the swing path will slightly pass over the ball because the body is stiffened without realizing it. If the tee is low at that time, there is a high probability of topping.

In addition, most amateurs raise their upper body while swinging, and no one plays lower than at address, so raising the tee slightly higher when playing golf in the early morning when the body is not warm may yield better results.

However, if you raise the tee, people who normally slice a lot will likely get more slices, and people who have a bad hook will likely get more hooks, so you need to hit lightly while adjusting your strength. Golf is not decided until after 18 holes, so risking everything on the first shot may be short temper because you still have lack of practice.

Now, take a deep breath, look at the direction again, and take your first hit lightly.

7. Papillon's Escape

After 13 years of suffering and sorrow on 'Devil's Island', he finally found freedom and shared life with everyone.

Even golf sometimes gets stuck in 'Devil's Island. In golf, a missed ball leaves a smooth path, sometimes into the forest, sometimes into a bunker, causing disappointment and sorrow.

But you have to come out of it. You have to go through the forest, find a little sunlight, break through the gap, and lift it high into the sky from a collapsed embankment and let it fall easily. However, the hole is still far away, and another trap lurks in golf. There is a sea beyond the mountains.

A. Escape from the Rough

Korean golf courses are usually created by carving out mountains, cutting down trees, and filling up valleys, so they not only have strong curves and many ups and downs, but also have rough areas covered with trees and many rocky slopes.

Therefore, once the ball enters the rough, not only is the flagpole not visible, but because there are many dogleg courses, it is difficult to get the ball on the green straight from the rough.

Lady golfers and senior golfers with relatively short shot distances still have a low probability of entering the rough, but among young students and amateur golfers in their youth, due to their immaturity in shots and the desire to hit long shots, they often slice and the ball curves into the mountains.

Professionals have a high fairway hit rate, and even if they get into the rough, they rarely go deep into the mountain while slicing like amateurs, so they can easily get out of the rough. However, amateurs are different.

Once you get into the rough, it is difficult to maintain your stance and steer through the gaps in the trees, so it is ultimately best to safely take it out to a nearby fairway. However, greed is difficult to suppress.

Amateur golf is about hitting through the trees toward the flagpole, but then falling into deeper rough and losing all the scores you've worked so hard to build up. Therefore, unless you are confident, you can only lose one point by using the widest space and hitting the fairway. If you are lucky and it is a middle hole, you can make a three-on one putt to get par.

As people live, sometimes misfortune happens to them. However, isn't it said that life itself is a cycle of joys and sorrows, and if you protect yourself by passing through difficult times wisely, you will be exhausted?

The same goes for golf. Even world-class professionals sometimes end up in the rough. The question at this time is how to deal with this. In that respect, it is no different from a bunker shot or a rough shot. If you are not confident, you have no choice but to hit the fairway and wait for the next time. If you try your last great shot today, the chances of success are low. These shots usually end in failure in all likelihood.

Usually, the difference between amateurs and professionals appears here, and the difference between beginners and experienced people also appears here. Therefore, at this time, an attitude of not overdoing things, an attitude of thinking about safety rather than distance, and the wisdom to look forward to the future are more necessary than anything else.

Also, it is sometimes difficult to find a ball that has entered the rough, so you have to look into the mountains or ridges, but there are times when you cannot find it. If you repeat this process not once or twice, but several times, you may get so tired that you will not be able to hit the ball again and end up making a mess.

Therefore, if you cannot find it within 3 minutes, taking the next action quickly and being considerate so as not to interfere with other people's play is also part of golf etiquette.

Therefore, when entering deep rough, regardless of the distance to the hole, you may need to hold a short iron rather than a long club and make a punch shot with a low trajectory or hit a high ball.

The most important thing is to calm your mind and not be greedy about the distance, but to exercise self-control to safely move to a wide fairway. If you are greedy and only aim for the green, you will fall into the trap of self-destruction as second and third rough awaits you. This is also a time when mind control is more desperately needed than technology.

B. Bunker of horror

John Daly and Constantino Rocca, tied on points at the 1995 British Open at St. Andrews, went into a four-hole playoff.

However, Rocca, who fell into the dreaded bunker in the 'Devil's 17th Hole', was unable to get the ball out in one shot, and after only 3 strokes, he ended up hitting a considerable distance from the hole, resulting in a triple bogey. The match ended in a one-sided victory for John Daly. Even world−class major players suffer like this when their ball falls into a bunker, so isn't it natural for amateurs to be afraid of bunkers?

Although he has only recently learned it, a young man who was considered a promising player because he hit longer shots than anyone else, often falls into fairway bunkers or bunkers around the green when he goes out on the field. And even if you hit it well and get out, there are often cases where your face turns red because you can't reach the distance to hole.

However, watching pros save par by brilliantly sticking a ball that went into a bunker to the side of the hole, and then seeing a ball hit from a bunker go into the cup and come from behind to win, it seems that bunkers are not just objects of fear.

The problem is that although bunker shots, like tee shots and approach shots, need to be developed through separate techniques and practice, no matter which practice range you go to, not only is there no place to practice bunker shots, but even on regular mats, sand wedges are used. It is rare to see amateurs practicing shots with a sand wedge.

The existence of bunkers is essential in the design of a golf course, and the arrangement, shape, and location of the bunkers indicate the characteristics of the golf course, so research on the bunkers themselves and practice of bunker shots are absolutely necessary for improving golf skills. Therefore, while learning golf, I believe that your skills will improve if you boldly use shots that try to go over bunkers rather than hitting shots avoiding bunkers, and if you continue to make efforts to save par by using bunker shots without fear even if you fall into a bunker.

Even if you hit the ball while avoiding the

bunkers, it is difficult to avoid the dozens or even 100 bunkers throughout the 18 holes. As your handicap goes down.

So, when the bunker shot gradually goes as planned, you will break away from fear and become calm, no different from hitting a regular green.

Of course, there are large bunkers covered with sand, but usually there are fairway bunkers, cross bunkers, and guard bunkers around the green, which are not very deep. Among them, the garrison bunker or pot bunker is a bunker that is rarely seen in Korea, but in foreign countries it goes almost deep enough to reach the human eye. Therefore, it is important to use the sand wedge well, which has been developed as a necessary tool for these bunker shots.

In addition, people who know how to skillfully use a sand wedge usually have a good swing form and are good at tee shots and other shots, so I would like to boldly recommend the use of a sand wedge.

Also, since the sand wedge is not only used for bunker shots, you will not be able to improve your skills without separately practicing this unique club, and it will not help you score.

And since sand wedges are often used for short-distance approach shots and can be used for a variety of purposes, if you continue to practice at a range of 10 to 70 meters, your score will change noticeably. Now, the shortcut to becoming 'low-handy' is to not only practice the driver but also spend a certain amount of time practicing the sand wedge.

C. Slice and hook

After starting to play golf, most players begin to worry about slices and then hooks. There are also opposite cases, though.

I've swung the golf club thousands of times, but the ball keeps bending to the right and sometimes to the left, which is unfortunate and often makes me worry because it's not easy to fix. Moreover, the stronger a young beginner is, the more likely it is that the ball will not fly straight.

So, if the ball goes out to OB or is sliced and goes into the bushes, you will lose all the scores you worked so hard to earn. And If you can't make a bogey, let alone a par, on the next hole and the following next hole, the day's golf is likely to be a mess.

If you look at professional technical books, you will hear countless reasons for slices, but you cannot know what causes slices, and even if you know, it is common for them to not be corrected right away and to repeat themselves.

In this case, you can't help but exclaim as you go to a nearby practice range, keep hitting practice balls, and feel confident that you've caught a certain number of slices. Then, when you go out to the field, you'll get slices once or twice again.

The same goes for the professional world. There are cases where the front runner's tee shot in the 17th and 18th holes of the final round misses the championship by missing the fairway, entering the rough, or falling into a bunker. What about amateurs? In that respect, we should rather take comfort.

Of course, we will have to start with the basic form to correct whether it is a slice or a hook. This is especially true for younger golfers. As you get older and gain more experience, your body becomes hard and it is difficult to correct your form, so it is usually just a temporary stopgap measure.

The more problematic thing is that it is not

just one type of slice or hook, but sometimes slices and sometimes hooks are mixed together. Because you can't trust the direction of your ball, you become confused and don't know which way to hit the ball.

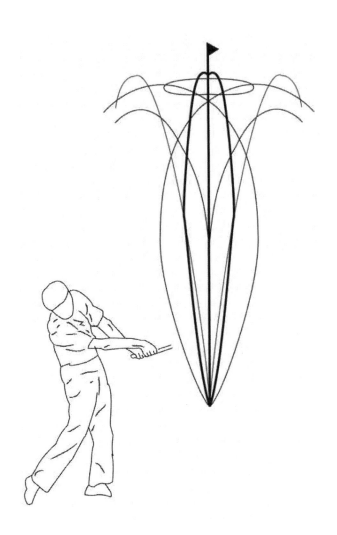

However, in most cases, once you hit a certain point, whether it is a slice or a hook, it is biased to one side, so you only need to correct that point. Of course, it is rare for a golf ball to fly in a straight line, and although there is a difference in degree, it is bound to fly deviated to the right or left.

It can be a hook or a slice, but if you make a planned shot, it can be a fade ball or a draw ball. Some players mainly play draw balls or fade balls, while others can use both at will.

However, in the case of an average golfer, it is common for a slice or hook to occur for a certain period of time, and once the basic form hardens, it almost always hardens to a slice or hook. In that case, if possible, developing it into a draw ball or fade ball and making it your own way will greatly help your score.

Ben Hogan rose from illness, came back a year later, and swept the tournament to immortalize himself. When reporters asked him for his secret, the secret he revealed three years later was very simple. Ben Hogan once revealed that he adjusted the direction depending on whether he placed his left thumb in the correct position on the shaft and hit straight, slightly to the left and hit a fade ball, or to the right and hit a draw ball.

If an amateur golfer is confident about hitting a fade ball, he or she should aim for the left side of the fairway, and if he or she is hitting a draw ball, he or she can aim for the right side of the fairway and use twice as much area as when aiming directly at the middle of the fairway. Therefore, the probability of hitting OB is reduced accordingly, and you can hit with confidence, so the distance is usually greater.

Moreover, the stance position of the teeing ground is not flat depending on the location, and the fairway is in various states such as uphill, downhill, right slope, left slope, etc. depending on the location, so it is difficult to adjust the direction with the stance, so the left side is difficult to control. It's very easy to adjust with just one thumb. When I go out on the field, I have often achieved good scores by taking full advantage of Ben Hogan's secret. I recommend you give it a try.

D. Prevention of topping

It is common to see a ball that is swung with all its might on a rainy afternoon in the field, but instead of rising, it just slips and stops after less than 100m.

This topping phenomenon, which is especially common in beginners who have just learned the golfer or lady golfers who lack strength, is a phenomenon that occurs when the clubhead hits the top of the ball, and is a bad hit that results from not meeting the ball accurately. However, the topping phenomenon that occurs frequently in the beginning makes the player anxious, and it is inevitable that topping continues with subsequent hits.

These toppings aren't just for beginners. Even players who are said to be pretty good at hitting can sometimes experience this on a tiring afternoon, so it's worth thinking about how to overcome it. This topping phenomenon, which is often seen in lady golfers, can be seen as stemming from the nature of women who are relatively more considerate but more vulnerable than men.

It feels good to be out in the silky fields for the first time, or once or twice a month at best, and often hitting the cheek lightly for fear of damaging the grass leads to topping, which is in contrast to the rugged nature of the men.

When you watch the fairway shots of many professional golfers on TV, you often see fist-sized lumps of dirt flying away with the golf ball, but amateur golfers don't even dare to do that. And even if you make up your mind, when you go out on the field, you end up hitting the ball slightly and topping it repeatedly.

In addition, most early amateur golfers forget that they should hit the right side of the ball because it is customary to look directly above the ball and hit it.

Even if it is a fairway, when the grass is not mowed the day after it rained or when you enter the rough, only the top half of the ball is visible and in reality, it is usually several centimeters deep into the grass. If you repeat the shot without taking this into account, it can cause a missed shot. It will happen.

Therefore, when you are in a situation like this, you must boldly hit the ball from the right side, and only by hitting with a down blow will the ball rise high and fly the intended distance. Since the ball is stuck, if you hit it with an upper blow as if it is floating, or if you only look at the top of the ball and hit it without considering the locked part, you will continue to topping.

Paradoxically, hitting the right side of the ball as if hitting it backwards can be a means of preventing topping.

These amateurish mistakes are not explained in detail in general textbooks and do not often come up when practicing on the practice field, so it is not easy to be embarrassed when you go out into the actual field. However, let's calm down and improve our posture to avoid repeating it twice.

E. Throwback and aerial ball

In golf, a duff, or a flop, is a typical golf miss shot. In the early days of learning how to play golf, when practicing on the field, you may have had the embarrassing experience of wondering why a club that hit well on the practice range would often hit the wrong side of the fairway. Especially when the wind is strong and the club is swung uphill or downhill, the club often falls over, revealing the beginner's inexperience.

On the other hand, aerial balls, or flops, often occur late in the round, even for people who have been playing golf for a long time. This is especially common in wet fields on rainy afternoons. This can often be seen in elderly people who have lost their energy due to age or female golfers who are weak, and they suffer huge losses in distance.

If you hold the club for a long time and hit it, it will fly a lot only if you hit it well, and if you hold the club for a long time, it will be difficult to control the golf club.

Compared to a duff, a flop, or aerial ball, is mainly a miss shot caused by only downswing and omitting the follow—through, i.e the post—swing action. It often occurs when hitting on wet grass in the latter half of the round or immediately after rain.

Even in this case, the best short—term solution is to let go of the desire for distance, hold the club as short as possible, and strengthen control. In addition, in order to increase control in a situation where your strength is already low, you need to swing more slowly to increase the probability of hitting the ball accurately.

Even if you keep hitting with a long grip on the club to make up for the distance you once lost, as long as there is a problem with your swing form, the flop cannot be easily corrected, so you will repeat missed shots. Let' s hold the club briefly and hit it.

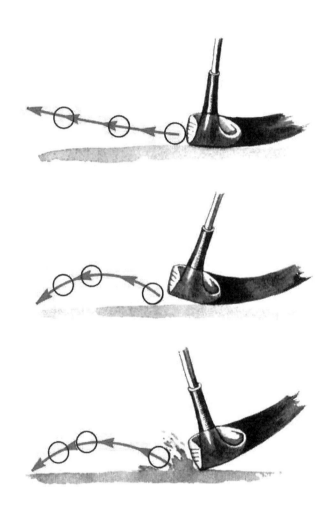

8. The flight of the eagle

An eagle flying in the sky.

It spreads its wings and spins around, glaring at the target in the valley. The majesty, openness, and sharp eyes. It measures a certain distance and flies freely in directions north, south, east and west, and when it finds its target, it comes down quickly.

In golf, when you can see the hole, you enter an emergency situation to capture it at all costs.

Measure the hole north, south, east, west, and look for a landing point by measuring the distance. If you don't approach correctly, the golf ball will fall in the wrong place. Sometimes you climb up, sometimes you go back to avoid the bunker.

A. Distance to hole

There is a significant difference in the distance to the hole from the champion tees and the regular tees, and the rule is that the distance from the lady tees is shorter. In Supplementary

Provision I−C of the Golf Rules, for men, the distance for a par 3 is 229 m (250 yards) or less, a par 4 is 230 m to 430 m (251 yards to 470 yards), and a par 5 long hole is 431 m (470 yards) or longer. The principle is that it is determined as follows.

However, since most courses measure distance horizontally from the center of the teeing ground to the center of the putting green, the actual shot distance can be said to vary when going uphill or downhill.

Korea's golf courses, which were created by demolishing mountains, have more ups and downs and steeper slopes than those in other countries, making it relatively more difficult to measure the distance when actually hitting a shot.

Usually, uphill holes are short and downhill or flat holes are relatively long, so if you look down on the distance because it is short, you may end up in unexpected trouble. In the case of pros, the tee shot distance can be said to be the first condition for score making because the average tee shot must be shot around 270 yards and the tee shot must be aimed at the green by approaching with an iron from there.

8. The flight of the eagle   117

It is a special case when Corey Pavin or Gary Player, who are relatively behind in distance, use an exquisite approach shot to put a chill on the nerves of a long hitter, and because a refreshing driver shot promises a good start, we become so absorbed in the tee shot and struggle to hit it even an inch farther.

However, golf, which started in the middle of life, is unlikely to be a good fit, and moreover, golf, which was learned late after working all of one's life without playing similar hitting sports such as baseball or tennis in the past, is considered good if you can hit 200 meters. Even when shooting 200m, depending on the course, there is still more than 180m left in the middle hole, and furthermore, if there is a bunker or water in front of the hole, taking a second shot is a burden for weekend golfers.

B. Zigzag strategy

Zigzag strategy How to attack the course is a matter of decision taking into account various factors such as course conditions, weather, and course design that day. No matter how good your swing is, the score usually varies greatly depending on the strategy.

I have seen many cases where even world-class pros do not use a strategy that suits their conditions that day, but rely only on their good performance until yesterday and try the same strategy today, only to fail without scoring any points.

The problem is that as humans, our conditions change morning and evening, and as our biorhythm changes, our swing form is affected and our shots change as well.

If you are a professional, you can compensate for this with long experience and daily training, but in the case of amateurs, the ball does not fly to the target accurately because the body does not listen. In other words, there are relatively more poorly hit and unsatisfactory balls than well-hit balls, which often ruins the day's score. So wasn't amateur golfer supposed to reduce miss shots? There are many cases. So wasn't amateur golfer supposed to reduce miss shots?

In this case, even if the ball goes wrong, is there a way to at least block the OB and prevent it from going into the bunker?

At this time, I would like to recommend the zigzag method. Unless you can hit all of your shots accurately as if measured by a ruler, you should set intermediate goals using a zigzag method before arriving at the hole. This is especially recommended for high handicappers with short distances.

For example, if you are not confident about two — on in a middle hole or if there is a bunker in front of the hole, it is worth trying the zigzag method because it reduces the risk even if you make a miss shot. The point is that in a 400m middle hole, if there is a bunker on the right side of the hole, if you hit your approach shot from the left, the probability of entering the bunker is reduced accordingly.

Therefore, it is advantageous to attack the shot before the approach shot by shooting from right to left. Of course, if there is a cross bunker or fairway bunker on the left, you must get out of the way.

In other words, if you are not confident about two-on and have decided to go three-on, it is often advantageous to attack the course by taking a tee shot from left to right, a fairway shot to the left, and an approach to the right.

It is common for most amateur golfers to hit the ball straight toward the hole when it lands in or near the right rough, then fall into the rough two or three times, resulting in a double or triple bogey. At that time, it is much better to hit it to the left, land it in the fairway, and make an approach shot from there.

A short-distance approach cannot necessarily be seen as advantageous. Which is more accurate: 100m approach or 70m approach? And what about 30m and 50m? There is no guarantee that the short approach is accurate. Let's boldly use the zigzag strategy.

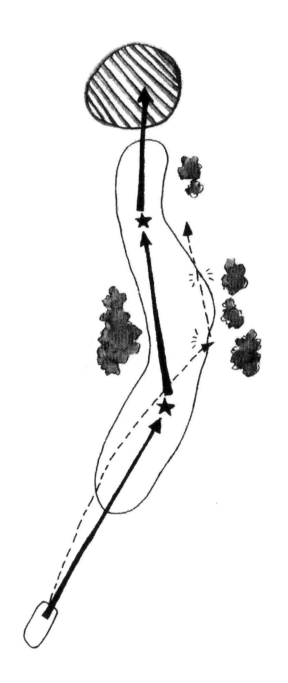

C. Strategy on the Green

The key to an approach shot is to place the ball in a good place for putting when hitting the putting green.

However, in reality, it is not only difficult for amateurs to get the ball on the green, but even if they do get the ball on, they are often at a distance from the hole.

No matter how good you are at putting, you have to get it close to the hole to finish with 2 putts. If you put the ball too far over the pin or on a downhill slope, putting is often difficult.

In cases like Korea, where climate changes are severe during the spring and summer, and two greens are used to protect the grass in the winter, the curves of the greens are still relatively gentle.

In foreign countries, there are cases where a single green is used, so the green at this time is usually 2 or 3 tiers and has severe curves back and forth, making it quite difficult for first-time golfers.

Also, even in Korea, where two greens are used, the green shape and situation are very different depending on the course, so the strategy is bound to vary depending on where the pin is inserted.

In general, putting greens are several tens of meters long and wide, so the overall area is quite large, and although it appears to be flat, it is very curved, so it is often difficult to clearly see the situation around the hole cup at first unless you play the course often.

In addition, since the pin's position divides the green into four parts and creates holes in the front, back, left and right, there is bound to be a difference in distance depending on the pin's position. In severe cases, it often exceeds 20 to 30 m, so the distance is measured based on the center of the green when approaching. Appropriate distance markings must be taken into account.

Normally, if there is a white stake or tree planted 100m ahead and the pin is behind it, 10m must be added to it to make it 110m. If it is planted in front, it must be adjusted to 90m, so there is a distance difference of about 20m, so check where the pin is placed and make your approach. Should be.

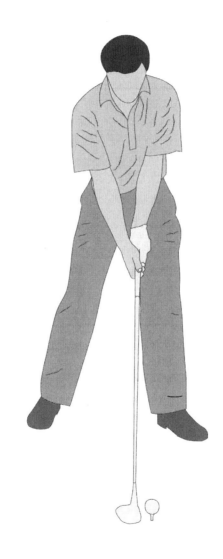

In addition, since the rolling distance of the ball varies depending on the weather conditions of the day, you must be able to handle the same distance according to the situation at that time, such as holding one club longer right after it rains in the summer, and holding the club shorter to account for the run on a clear fall day. You can hit the early 80s, and as the probability of hitting increases, you can hit the 70s.

If you watch TV, you can't help but be amazed when you see American PGA pros keeping their approach distances close and slightly leaning to either the left or right, making it a one-putt or two-putt. And in some cases, backspin is applied to the ball, causing it to return 2 to 3 meters and hitting it close to the pin in front of the green on the other side of the water. Not only is it almost magical, but it also shows that only by doing so can one rise to the top of the world. Realized.

As an average golfer, imitating their skills may be a bit daunting, but wouldn't it be fun for young golfers looking to hit 70 and fierce golfers with innate talent to not hesitate to hone their skills and try to improve their scores?

D. Blind spot of approach shot

You hit a thrilling tee shot at best of 200m and smiled in conversion, but the second shot sometimes went over the green to the right or left, and sometimes fell into a bunker before the distance at all, causing confusion on the approach shot. This happens often.

In comparison, it is surprising to see pros hitting the pin with a 6 or 5 iron from a distance of 180 to 200 yards.

But it is not something to be discouraged. Even on the world-famous US PGA Tour, most of the players who fail to be among the leaders and hit over par are usually left behind due to problems with the accuracy of their approaches.

The difference between a beginner and an experienced player can be determined by whether or not they are good at making approach shots. In the case of beginners, most of them only practice tee shots at the driving range and do not practice approach shots much, so even after hitting a great long shot, they often get exhausted because they have a hard time getting to the green.

Except for single-digit handicappers, it is not so common for weekend golfers to go two-on on middle holes and three-on on long holes. Even in the case of single handicappers, it is common to see a few mistakes and missed shots.

Therefore, there is no need to be disappointed if you do not have regular on. It is common for young long hitters to hit a great tee shot but have difficulty with a short approach, which means that it is difficult to match long and short distances.

The problem is that the obsession with having to hit the pin with the approach shot, as well as on the green, not only causes mistakes, but there is also the possibility of a 3-putt if you don't actually hit the pin, so the approach often determines the score.

A friend I know usually sets the ball at 70 to 80 yards for fairway shots and approaches the green from there. Not only am I confident in my approach from this distance by practicing with a pitching wedge or a No. 9 iron during my daily practice, but when I get close to the green, most of the time, the line or posture of the ball is not good, so it is difficult to hit and more finesse is required, so I prefer 30 yards. The strategy is to avoid the 40-yard approach.

8. The flight of the eagle   129

In comparison, one cannot help but be amazed at how a skilled golfer who uses exquisite approach shots puts the ball near the edge of the green and approaches with a one putt distance.

As your skills improve, your approach skills increase, and as various skills such as pitching, lobing, and bunker shots develop, your handiness goes down. When you play more holes and your score improves, the joy is greater than with a long shot. Adds a new taste.

Now, when you go to the practice range, put your driver aside for a moment and focus more on approach shots within 100 yards with a short iron. And let's attach it to the pin.

E. Short game around the green

Unlike professionals, it is difficult for most amateur golfers to get on the green regularly, so their score on the day often depends on how they handle balls that fall around the green.

Originally, young golfers show off their skills by using their strength to swing long shots 250 to 260 yards, but approach shots aimed at the green often miss, so it takes time to hit both long and short shots evenly.

If you are single-handed, you can easily get regular ons, but weekend golfers who usually hit in their 80s only occasionally get regular ons, and often hit the ball over, undershot, or miss, so skills around the green are especially required.

The problem is that when the ball lands within 20 to 30 meters around the green, the score of the day depends on how you handle it and save par.

Beginners are usually so focused on tee shots that they have no time to worry about close-range short games, so it is common to accidentally hit a ground ball or overshoot the green and make a mistake in one or two shots, and it is a common occurrence. The problem and difficulty faced by golfers in their 80s is that even low-handiness golfers are unable to hit the hole and hit the ball from more than 4 to 5 meters away, making it virtually difficult to save par.

The problem is that these close-range shots require somewhat modified shots, unlike tee shots or fairway shots. This requires a lot of experience and sense in pitching, running, pitch and run, and lob shots.

However, not only do people neglect their daily practice for close-range shots, but there are few practice centers that teach them accurately, so they think they have no choice but to go out into the field and learn it on their own, and through trial and error, it is inevitable that it will cost time and money to acquire the skill.

Many golfers who boast of strength are weak at close range shots like this. However, this technique, or minor technique, that requires extreme savings of strength and rhythm may be better suited for women or older golfers.

As you gradually learn about golf and realize that not everything can be solved by strength, and by the time you break through your 90s and look towards your 80s, it is impossible to enter your 80s without developing these skills.

And because the area around the green is the worst managed area, the lie of the ball is unstable and the undulation of the grass is the most severe.

Therefore, since golf skills require the most detailed and careful play, if you do not harmonize the club you use and the shot method well, it will be difficult to avoid playing poorly in the B class for the rest of your life.

This is also true for professionals. However, in the case of professionals, the purpose is different compared to amateurs, such as getting closer to the hole, and in some cases, trying to chip in and aiming for the winning shot. It is no different from amateurs in that the results vary depending on how skillfully the close shots are made.

The reason why senior golfers, who are generally unable to hit long shots like they did when they were younger due to weakened strength, demonstrate excellent ability in attacking the bottom of the green is because they have learned the wisdom to make up for short tee shot distances by using their long experience and sense.

So, people in their 20s, 30s, and 40s can play the game evenly, and even if parents, sons, and sons-in-law in their 60s and 70s play together, the score is difficult to determine the winner because close shots act as a buffer.

Therefore, if you become familiar with the short game, you will be able to feel its charm and reach a deeper level. Now, let's practice again starting from the 10-yard approach using a sand wedge, pitching wedge, and 9, 8, and 7 iron rather than a drive.

F. Short hole strategy

Regardless of the golf course, out of 18 holes, there are usually 4 long holes, 4 short holes, and the remaining 10 holes are middle holes.

It is common for pros to get a birdie in the long hole and to play the middle hole with a two-on and one-putt or two-putt depending on the situation. However, in short holes based on one on two-putt, you often have to be satisfied with par because you have to use only accurate tee shots and putts, and if you make a birdie in a short hole, your score that day will be good. When playing bogey, it is normal to show a lack of control.

In the case of amateurs, it is difficult to save par in short holes, and bogeys or double bogeys are often made, and the score in short holes often determines the score that day.

This is because the short hole does not allow for even a single poor miss shot, and if amateurs accidentally end up in a guard bunker or rough, it is difficult for amateurs to get out, so it is common for them to easily lose a point or two.

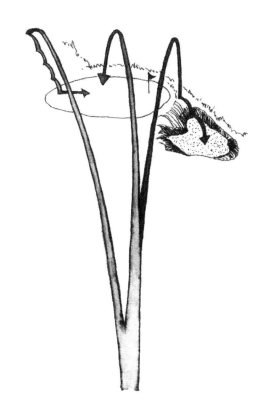

Most courses have bunkers around the short holes and the green itself is often an embankment green, so if the direction is slightly off or the distance is measured incorrectly, it is difficult to get on the green, and even if it is on, it is not only difficult to get on the hole. It is true that it is difficult to handle it with a one-putt because the distance is long.

Therefore, in the case of amateurs, it is common for average golfers to fall in front of the green or miss the distance.

Moreover, since the area around the green is the least well-maintained area, the grass is not in good condition, so even approach shots often result in missed shots. So, experts recommend that in short holes, if possible, hold the club as long as possible and hit with 80% force.

However, since the longest distance of a short hole is 250 yards (229m) for men and 210 yards (192m) for women, depending on the course, there are some holes that cannot be reached even if you hit a driver, so in these cases, you have no choice but to go for a two-on. There is no, and you must approach it the same way as the middle hole.

However, in most regulars, the green is

usually at one-on distance, so you need to pay special attention to which club to choose, and most of the short holes are located in a downward or upward direction, so the wind blows and it is difficult to determine the direction. There are many places that require it.

Depending on the location, there are a lot of people crowded around the short hole, so players who are weak-minded may be conscious of the crowd and miss shots at the short hole.

In the end, it is common for people who know how to attack short holes to play well that day and achieve excellent scores in score making. A place that should not be neglected is the short hole.

9. Eagle's Claw

Those sharp claws of the flying eagle.

The eagle snatches its prey with its claws and returns to its nest. Once caught in those claws, it is difficult for any animal to escape. Moreover, if you grab it and fly into the sky, the ground beast will not be able to use its limbs.

Once you find your goal, the hole, you have to do whatever it takes to get it.

Now I'm wondering what to do with it. I have fourteen weapons. In it, 7th, 8th, and 9th times, sometimes pitching or sand wedges are brought out. And the person who catches the hole wins.

So, we do everything we can to get it as close to the hole as possible and to attach it to the pin as much as possible.

A. Choice of iron and wood

Even if beginners practice hard with wooden clubs, they usually practice relatively little iron shots. Even if I practice iron shots, I only practice short irons or middle irons if I'm good at it, and I rarely practice long irons because they don't work well even if I practice.

The reason is that it is difficult to use long irons, and you have to be in your 80s to use long irons freely.

If you look at pros, they usually use long irons at a distance of around 200 yards and lower their scores by putting them on or close to the green.

However, for amateurs, using a long iron when the tee shot distance is not correct may be beyond their ability. Therefore, by using baffy or cleek instead of long iron to gain distance, and by using it habitually, you naturally develop the habit of staying away from long irons.

However, even if you are a strong male or female golfer, it is only a shortcut for a fierce golfer aiming to be in your 80s or younger to skip the long iron without using it, and you should use it boldly and get used to it.

Short irons and middle irons are relatively short, so they are easy and comfortable to handle, but long irons have small lofts and are long, so even if they are hit, it is difficult to get the direction and distance exactly right.

However, compared to wood, there are many amateurs who use it because it is more accurate when hit, and recently, many clubs designed to be easy to hit have come out, so they are not necessarily difficult to handle.

However, it is true that it is difficult for amateurs to handle the 2nd and 3rd irons, let alone the 1st iron, so the 1st and 2nd irons are often excluded from the set from the beginning.

On the other hand, the 6th and 7th woods are available to cover the distance of long irons and provide accuracy that is comparable to that of long irons, which is fortunate for golfers with weak strength.

Compared to long irons, middle irons are not only easier to handle but also have greater accuracy, so you should use them for approaches facing the pin and use short irons at shorter distances for greater accuracy.

The problem at this time is the distance of the

iron.

It varies from person to person, but you should be careful when choosing a club by knowing your shot distance to some extent accurately.

B. How to use short iron

When covering distances of less than 100m and approaching around the green, the short iron can be said to play a key role in score making, just like the putter.

Not only is it difficult for most average golfers to hit the green regularly, but in long holes, the third stroke is often approached within 100m, so the method of determining the distance and direction and approaching the hole cup is It can be said that they vary greatly.

The reason why there are many cases where a long hitter hits a great tee shot and fairway shot, then comes around the green and fails the approach shot, and is caught by a short hitter who hits step by step, is because there is a problem with the handling of the short iron.

In general, the reason why sluggers are

strong at creating distance but weak at hitting the ball lightly at close range is because the short iron is not hit only with force.

For example, even with the same pitching, some people can reach 120 meters, while others can hit only 70 to 80 meters, so the key is which pitcher you hit with.

There are usually bunkers around the green or the entire green is a turret green, so if it is not an accurate shot, it is often difficult to put even if it is on, and depending on the shape of the green, if you put on the spot for a downhill putt, the next turn is often very difficult.

The more experienced a player is, the better he or she is at handling short irons, sand wedges, and pitching wedges, and he/she uses various shots such as bunker shots, pitch shots, and lob shots to overcome crises and successfully save par. thus reducing his score.

As the handicap decreases, the handling of these short shots improves, and as a result, the score decreases. As a result, the desire for unreasonable long shots disappears, and the player reaches the point of being honest and trying to do everything as it should, allowing him to enjoy the pleasure of golf even more. Short shot! Let's pay more attention.

C. Use of the 7 iron

It is not easy for an amateur golfer to use all 14 golf clubs perfectly. Young people become obsessed with drivers and long irons out of a desire to hit long shots, and as they get older, their strength weakens, so they use wood more often on the fairway. Lady golfers do not have the right physique to begin with, so they attack holes with wood. do.

Therefore, even if you go out on the field with all 14 clubs, it is rare to use the clubs appropriately depending on the situation, and at the end of the game, there are some clubs that have never been used.

Each person has their own preferred club. Since everyone has different physique and different strengths, there are naturally clubs that suit them well and clubs that do not. So, you have to choose the one that suits you best.

In these cases, the 7 iron can be said to be the most suitable.

Among the 9 iron clubs ranging from 3 to sand wedge, the 7 iron is in the middle, and is located in the middle in terms of distance and loft, so it has various uses.

Among average golfers, it is common to be able to hit 120–150m with a 7–iron, and even lady golfers can hit 90–120m, so the score can vary greatly depending on the use of the 7–iron.

In addition, it can be used for pitch shots and running approaches by taking advantage of the loft around the green, so it can be used for a variety of purposes. It is also suitable for when the ball is lost in the rough and when you need to get the ball out between the trees. Amateurs need to use and practice the 7 iron intensively.

Among average golfers, it is common to be able to hit 120–150m with a 7–iron, and even lady golfers can hit 90–120m, so the score can vary greatly depending on the use of the 7–iron.   In addition, it can be used for pitch shots and running approaches by taking advantage of the loft around the green, so it can be used for a variety of purposes. It is also suitable for when the ball is lost in the rough and when you need to get the ball out between the trees.

Amateurs need to use and practice the 7 iron intensively.

D. Use of Sand Wedge

The sand wedge was probably made to literally knock the ball out of the sand of a bunker.

If there was no sand wedge, not only would it be virtually impossible to hit the ball out of a bunker as deep as 1 to 2 meters, but the enjoyment of golf would also be halved.

In the 1995 British Open, John Daly escaped danger by hitting the ball out of a bunker in the fourth round, while Constantino Rocco collapsed in a bunker even after going into overtime.

Also, Paul Azinger, who swept the PGA Championship in the United States in 1993, hit a bunker shot that will go down in history, and Bob Tway, who won the PGA Championship in 1986, also hit a bunker shot that will go down in history. He won 4 times that year and became PGA Player of the Year by cupping Greg Norman with a wonderful bunker shot on the last hole.

This magical record was made possible by the presence of a sand wedge. Therefore, as the handicap decreases, the golfer should not neglect practicing bunker shots with a sand wedge.

Gary Player's bunker shots were so accurate that Arnold Palmer once confessed that he wished his ball had not ended up in the bunker.

In general, amateur golfers are afraid of bunkers, so not only do they neglect to practice bunker shots from the beginning, but once the ball enters the bunker, they hit it with a feeling of giving up and are unable to improve their skills.

It is difficult to explain this bunker shot in one word, but you must master the technique by thoroughly practicing the basics of opening the club face, putting your weight on your left foot, and hitting it with a half swing without rushing.

It goes without saying that you should use a sand wedge in a bunker. So are sand wedges only used in bunkers? Of course, as an average golfer, excluding beginners, there is no way he would not know that the sand wedge is just as useful as the pitching wedge in the short game.

Corey Pavin, who came to Korea, used a sand wedge from 100 yards and hit the shot almost on the hole cup, which is one of the common techniques not only among pros but also low handicappers.

The problem is that long hitters usually reduce their scores by attempting an approach using a sand wedge at 100 meters, but how do they handle it at the shortest distance of 20 to 50 meters?

It is usually easy for strong young people to hit with all their might, but it is often relatively more difficult to relax and hit lightly.

Therefore, it is not only the case of amateur golfers who cannot hide their disappointment when the ball within 50m unexpectedly misses the target and deviates significantly from the hole cup.

Not only are golfers with long experience generally good at handling these short distances, but it is also common for them to use a sand wedge or pitching wedge to hit the pin at a one-putt distance, confusing the person who came to the green early.

Therefore, we realize that the sand wedge is not a special tool used only in bunkers, and that it is a tool that can reduce scores by actively using it in short approaches, so why not find a way to actively use it and contribute to score making?

E. Benefits of Clique

Cleek, or Wood No. 5. The 5—wood with a loft of 22° and a shaft length of 40.5 inches is the most useful wood for average amateur golfers.

Unlike the pros, the driver shot distance is not long enough and therefore when it is not possible to easily reach the green in a middle hole with an iron, the clique is not only used as a replacement, but is also useful for fairway shots in long holes, and sometimes in the rough or in the cross on the fairway. It can also be used in cross bunkers, making it an all—purpose club.

In general, amateur golfers often have to attempt an approach with a long iron because their tee shot distance is much shorter than that of a professional golfer. However, long irons are harder to use than expected and it is difficult to accurately hit the sweet spot on the fairway. Therefore, using Clique at this time can greatly alleviate the difficulty.

The loft is similar to the 3—iron's 23°, so not only does the ball fly well, but the distance is also greater than that of the 3—iron, so it is often used.

Moreover, in the fall and winter, when the grass dies and the ground is almost bare, using wood, especially clique, is much more effective than using iron.

It is also used as a tool to save par by using a clique from a bunker when there is a considerable distance left to the green, often hitting the green a distance of 150 to 160 m.

In addition, in the case of elderly golfers who have lost their strength or lady golfers who are relatively weaker than men, it is sometimes better to hit a tee shot with a spoon or clique instead when the driver is not good, rather than blindly holding the driver.

The problem is that you need the courage to throw away the driver and grab the clique. However, since most golfers insist on using the driver, they often end up making a series of missed shots.

Compared to an iron, the characteristic of a click is that the ball makes more runs after hitting the ground. Therefore, when approaching the ball to the green, it is necessary to take this into account and take into account the distance it will roll to the pin after dropping it in front of the green.

Of course, at this time, if you can freely use irons 3 and 4, it is much more advantageous to hit iron shots. However, since most average amateur golfers are inexperienced in using long irons, it can be said that if you get used to it by using the clique without having to forcefully hold the iron, your shots will become smoother and your score will improve, which is a win—win. Let's actively use Clique.

10. On the Heavenly sea

A quiet sea-like lake located on the peak of MT. Baekdu in north Korea. A place everyone wants to visit at least once in his life.

The sea surrounded by rocks on all sides and the calm waves on it. Whether it rains or snows, the sea embraces everything without saying a word. However, even here, there is a breath of waves and mystery, so we naturally bow our heads.

After going through all the hardships and reaching the green, We feel like we have reached the top of the mountain. Now, we calm down, count with our eyes all around the hole and since we are afraid of losing the hole, we wander around the hole.

Suddenly silence prevails. People's breathing stops, and only the player's pulse fluctuates. You've come a long way, but if you miss this hole it's a bogey, if you catch it, it's a birdie. we bet everything on this one hit.

A. Tragedy of "Head Up"

"Head up," is an advice on the field that a senior golfer politely gives to a new golfer. This 'head up' is usually heard when the ball is not hit at well.

The psychology of wanting to know the direction of the ball you hit at as soon as possible, as you are anxious that the ball may not fly in the wrong direction due to a swing you are not yet used to, causes you to miss the ball, leading to a 'ground ball' or 'slice' ball.

"Heads up" doesn't just mean raising your head. It is rather natural that due to the head—up, all movements are disturbed and the central axis of the swing collapses, so the ball deviates from the sweet spot and misses the direction.

Old golfers too sometimes do make "heads-up" However, it is common for people to get lost without knowing the cause of a missed shot because they are not sure whether they did heads-up or not.

If you looked at the shots of Corey Pavin and Tom Watson, who participated as invited players in the Slang-Raying Challenge golf tournament held in Korea, you could see that both of them kept their heads still for a considerable period of time after hitting the ball and only look straight down on the ground with their eyes.

In the end, swinging while looking straight at the spot where the ball is placed without turning your head up means that you can swing without disturbing the central axis of the swing, thereby enabling a stable circular motion and allowing the ball to be hit at the sweet spot of the club head and fly in the intended direction.

But what is the reason why this simple action is not followed? Of course, the direct cause is the impatience to see the direction the ball is flying, but fundamentally, it can be said that the bigger cause is the lack of basic exercises during regular swing practice time.

In all swing movements, proper rotation is

possible only when the center of gravity supporting the axis is stable

However, in the case of golf, it is said that the central axis is based on the spine, but the lower part is supported by both feet, so it is stable, but the head is not fixed, so the only way to overcome this is through his will and practice, because head movement is something that seems simple but is not simple.

In addition to this, long hitters want to see in advance how far the ball will fly, and beginners are worried that the ball will miss the poind and cause damage to the person next to them, so they usually head up, causing a miss shot and lowering the score of the day. resulting in ruining the score.

That's why Jack Nicklaus generally recommends starting your swing by intentionally turning your head slightly to the right, that is, looking at the back of the ball in a chin back state, and slowing down the backswing.

It is reasonable that once a ball is hit, it flies in the same state as it was hit. I tell myself in my mind, "If I see the ball flying far away after hitting the ball to make a great shot, it's not too late, so I don't go heads up this time!", but before I know it, I end up going heads up again. Is this really the habit of an amateur golfer?

B. Trap of "Never Up, Never In"

"Never up, never in" means that if you putt the ball from the green and it doesn't reach the hole, there is no chance of cupping the hole. This is the most commonly used saying in putting.

Therefore, in putting, it is generally emphasized to make a stroke that passes the hole. In fact, masters like Arnold Palmar are considered representative golfers who hit the ball past the hole when putting.

In theory, every shot must pass the hole to have a chance of making a hole-in, so it can be said that most amateurs also practice this way of putt. However, the problem is that not all balls passing through the hole does not fall into the hole.

Although the green appears to be flat, it is not only slanted back and forth and left and right, but also has several mounds around it, so there is a problem with the ball being putted not rolling as smoothly as we hit it on a mat at home. Not only that, but also most amateurs does not hit the ball almost every day. Unlike professionals, the problem is that they are not confident in their putt sense, so they do not have an accurate sense of distance.

Even in the case of pros, if the lie is uphill, they prefer to putt as far in front of the hole as possible during the approach shot, and make an uphill putt.

However, in the case of downhill putting, the ball slides and rolls due to natural gravity that cannot be controlled by human power, so not only is it difficult to accurately determine the rolling distance, but there is also a slope to either the left or right. you may deviate significantly from the target point and end up taking a fatal hit by 3-putting.

Therefore, even if the approached ball sticks to the fringe or edge, it is sometimes advantageous in terms of scoring to putt it close to the hole and cup it in with the next putt shot.

In fact, even world-class professionals average 1.7 to 1.8 in putting, succeeding with a one-putt about once in four or five times, and usually they are two-putting.

An example of a great putting on TV is showing the occasional long putt, but not showing the numerous balls that don't go in.

Therefore, except in exceptional cases where you are competing for a comeback victory with just one stroke, for example, when the line is more than 5m or very difficult, it is much wiser to prevent 3-putting by sticking close to the hole rather than letting it graze the hole.

Moreover, if you try to cup in recklessly and greedily even though you have no confidence in your ability due to lack of sense of your body not being warmed up, and you miss the subsequent shot and end up making a 3-putt, it may even affect the shot in the next hole and result in a huge loss.

Therefore, wouldn't it be safer to limit "Never Up Never In" to a safe distance of 5 to 6 meters, and in other cases, let us be satisfied with settling for a two putt by making it closer to the hole? Let go of greed. Amateurs!

C. The fun of putting

If you watch a golf match broadcast, of course tee shots and rough shots are shown, but most of the time is spent on putting on the green. Lots of spectators seats are also located next to the green, and the area around the green of the

18th and final hole is characterized by the crowds forming during famous matches.

On a par 72 regular course, putting accounts for the most shots, so victory or loss is often determined by the result of the putt. In the case of pros, most players make it to the green within the required number of strokes, and in long holes, there are cases where it is two-on, but victory or defeat is still determined by the putt.

In the 1989 Masters, Scott Hoch, who was leading, missed a 90cm short putt on the 17th hole and went into overtime, and missed a 60cm short putt in overtime too, missing a narrow victory, and ended up with the victory of persistent Nick. The reason he gave in to Nick Faldo was because of his poor putt.

Seeing how a seemingly simple putt can be the difference between winning and losing, it seems like there must be some knack to putting.

If you look at a technical book, there are several tips on putting listed, but putts vary greatly depending on the player, so it is impossible to say for sure that 'this is it.' In the end, it is left to each person's form, sense, and guts.

In fact, most amateurs not only do not have a

suitable place to practice putting, but they also do not have free time enough. So when they go to the practice range, they mostly focus on wood or iron shots and don't practice putting much.

Also, even if you practice putting, it doesn't seem like you'll improve much, and because the results vary greatly depending on the condition of the day and the texture of the grass, practicing doesn't seem to be of much use, so in the end, it seems like skill of putting improves depending on experience and experience. I also have doubts. However, if you want to build up a certain level of skill and raise your score to the 70s, you cannot help but pay attention to it even if the order of learning is late, because your putting technique decisively determines your score.

Moreover, when you need to prevent a double bogey or triple bogey and decisively hit it into the hole from a distance of 2 to 3 meters, you cannot neglect putting practice in order to feel the pleasure of hitting the ball with the determination to hit it.

Therefore, weekend golfers, housewife golfers who cannot go to the driving range often due to household chores, and golf manias who feel the inconvenience of having to go to the golf course or driving range every day even if they practice frequently, all have the same concerns how to do it. So It is common to practice on one mat at a time. However, due to monotony and standardized lines, skill development is not as exciting and fun as practice, so it usually does not go long.

The trick to putting lies in being able to hit it straight at a certain distance, and in addition, advanced skills are needed to judge the height by looking at the texture of the grass.

Therefore, you must learn and get a feel for the feeling and overcome it through constant effort and practice. To do this, you need to make the most of the mats you have at home.

Mats at home, which are usually only 5m long, do not sufficiently provide the sense of distance of 6m, 7m, 9m, 12m, or 15m. At this time, one way is to inflate the mat like ∩ and play it on a double green, so you can feel the distance a little bit sufficiently.

Depending on the degree of inflation, you can feel a distance of 5m, 7m, 9m, 12m, or even 15m, so if you practice at home for 10 or 20 minutes whenever you have time, you can learn the distance and feel the shot without much effort, which makes it even more fun. This is a method I would definitely recommend.

D. Prevention of three putts

How many putts will you make during 18 holes? If you finish with 2 putts per hole, it will be 36, which proves how important putts are as they account for half of the scores on a par 72 course.

There are many techniques related to putting that are professionally described in various technical books, but unlike the tee shot, the main point is that you should avoid heads up and hit with a pop or stroke according to each individual's personality.

However, the putt must be cupped into the hole, which is the final goal. In other words, because it is a decisive blow, it can be entered from more than 10m and cannot be entered from less than 1m, so it is literally a crossroads where the joy and evil hyperbolas are divided.

The essence of putting is ultimately to consider two things. One is to read the condition of the green and adjust the direction and distance of the ball, and the other is to hit the putting itself exactly as adjusted.

The first problem is reading the condition of the green. Not only is it difficult for most average golfers to accurately read the slopes, or inclinations, of the front, back, left, and right sides of the green, but also the condition of the greens varies in moisture and gloss depending on the morning and day, which can blind the eyes.

Of course, the most important thing at this time is whether the slope is uphill or downhill, and, depending on which side is higher on the left or right, the putting direction and distance can vary greatly.

Regardless of any other greens, no green is 100% flat, and the level of difficulty varies depending on the position of the flagpole, so the problem is that the state of the green can only be learned through experience.

In general, putts on the green are where beginners lose the most to experienced, and a professional golfer's win or loss is largely determined by putts.

Most amateur golfers initially neglect putting, which requires the most self-control and concentration compared to the splendor of the tee shot, but when they break 90 and hit 80, they realize the importance of putting, so they buy a mat at home and practice frequently. This is because we gradually realize that score making is impossible without good putting.

Then, the joy of going out on the field and finishing with 2 putts instead of 3 or 4 putts, and in some cases, getting a cup in with 1 putt is no different from the exhilaration of hitting a tee shot.

But the problem is how to finish in 1 or 2 putts and get rid of 3 putts. Usually it is okay to miss a birdie chance and end up with a bogey, or to fail to make a long putt of 10m or more into the hole cup and end up making 3 putts.

When a hole is made in a strange place with an uneven slope, there are times when you have no idea in which direction and with what force you should hit, so you end up making a 3-putt.

Moreover, on a seaside green, the ball flows towards the sea, making it difficult to determine the direction with just your eyes, so there are cases where you have to use a certain amount of feel to hit the ball.

Therefore, when it comes to putting, practice is more important than special instruction because each situation is different.

Even if you have a good look at the green, in order to put the ball in the hole cup, the second factor is that you have to have a good putting feel so that the ball rolls as planned and you make a hole-in.

In golf, it can be said that putting is the thing that most sensitively reflects the conditions of the day. The target range for tee shots and fairway shots is wide, so even on bad days, you can get by with it, but for putting, the target location is fixed and you have to cup in. That is why you feel stressed about having to hit it. Putting is also the best reflection of your condition after drinking and not sleeping well last night.

Sometimes, putting is also affected in many ways, such as stiff hands and shoulders after driving for 2-3 hours, or starting a round on a

Saturday afternoon without prior practice.

Therefore, pre-conditioning is more important than anything else, and when you get on the green without practice, it is best to remain calm and collected, and in the case of long putts, aim to putt within 1m around the cup and reduce the number of putts to 3.

Since the probability of 3 putts is greater than the probability of 1 putt, it can be said that giving up the greed for a birdie and having the composure to finish with 2 putts prevents miss shots and ultimately contributes to improving the score.

E. Par or Bogey

Birdie, par or bogey? When anyone grabs a golf club and goes out on the course to take a round, they usually start the round by secretly promising themselves that they will play well today and get a few birdies or pars.

Of course, a professional will make a desperate attempt to achieve a birdie or eagle in order to hit under par, but an amateur golfer will be satisfied with just a par, let alone a birdie or an eagle.

However, the problem is that even if most amateur golfers play well during a round, if they get OB in one or two places or are in the rough and hit a double bogey or triple bogey, and become discouraged, isn't it normal for them to ruin three or four holes in the blink of an eye? No, not only amateurs but also professional golfers are the same in that regard.

When you see Gil Morgan, who was leading in 1993 at the famous US Open, collapsed in the second half of the third round and was eventually trampled by Tom Kite, you feel an indescribable bitterness.

Is it just that?, In the 1989 British Open, when Calcavecchia, Wayne Grady, Greg Norman competed in a 4-hole playoff that went into overtime, Greg Norman, who was ahead by 2 holes, lost after 3 or 4 holes, making the viewer feel very sad.

To summarise In short, everyone, whether a professional or an amateur, decides to play well, but in reality, it is common for a birdie chance to turn into a bogey or a double bogey. The problem is how many ridiculous shots are repeated over the course of 18 holes. That's why it's said that golf is a sport that reduces actual hits as much as possible.

This is because not only technology but also psychological factors play a big role in producing such a hit. No matter how good a shot you make, a very small error at the moment of impact can spread to a distance of several meters or tens of meters 200 meters in front, so you are bound to make at least one or two mistakes that cannot be helped by human ability.

Even more so for amateur golfers. For an amateur golfer with an average score in the 80s, if he plays bogey, he gets 90, if he makes 9 pars, he gets 81, and to get in the 70s, he needs to get 11 or more pars.

Single handicappers hitting the 70s, so-called singles, are amateurs but usually live at the golf course or practice range. Therefore, it is virtually impossible for the average weekend golfer to hit 70s every time unless he or she is a genius. Therefore, wouldn't it be best for amateur golfers who want to enjoy the weekend by hitting the 80s at all costs to do their best to hit the 80s or even the low 80s?

Of course, there are extremes who hit their 70s, but how many amateur golfers are like that?

That's why we feel indescribably happy when we catch a birdie during the round, and when we happen to get an eagle, we get excited about planting trees around the green and giving our friend a nice treat. Looking at this, it can be seen that amateurs are not only concerned about the score, but also have a strong desire to hit one or two great shots and putts in a memorable way.

So, while aiming for a birdie, you end up with a bogey, and while aiming for an eagle, you end up in the rough, so your score does not easily improve.

Professionals who strictly manage their scores and amateurs who are greedy for hitting great shots. Isn't this why average golfers are always hovering in the 80s without improving their scores or skills?

11. Snows of Kilimanjaro

Kilimanjaro, located at the highest peak in Africa, is a spiritual peak that is better known to us through movies and novels. However, even though we just want to go there, the road is too rough and uncomfortable, so we take out the book again.

Anyone can go on a hiking course, but the mountain is too high and rough to reach the summit, so many people stay halfway. Among them, the path of the so-called 'single' golfer, who climbs the summit alone, is also a lonely path to the peak.

Everyone wants to play golf and play well, but not everyone is good at golf. Just like mountain climbing, you have to climb up and up while constantly avoiding dangers to become a so-called "single golfer.

A. Golfer's Conditions

It is generally said that in order to play golf well, you must be thorough in the 3C: concentration, control, and confidence.

The moment you pick up the club and stroke the ball, the most important thing is to throw away all distracting thoughts and concentrate your mind on sending the ball straight to the target.

However, this kind of mental concentration cannot be achieved without confidence in the swing and the certainty that the ball will be sent to the target point based on the skills and experience accumulated over the years.

In addition, it is only possible by using the club without being overly ambitious and using the skills you have honed over the years.

The stroke moment lasts only a few seconds. Out of the 4–5 hours it takes to play 18 holes, the time spent on actual strokes is only 7–8 minutes at most for average golfers. The score of the day depends on this short period of time. But the rest of the time to support the 7–8 minutes of stroke isn't just walking.

When you step on the teeing area, you must judge the overall situation of the course, that is, look at the direction, undulation, bushes, wind direction, etc. to select an accurate target point and predict the ball's trajectory before making a stroke. Measure the distance on the fairway as well. You must constantly focus your mind on preliminary movements for the next shot by checking the location of the bunker, rough, and mound, catching your breath, and accurately judging the clock and adjusting your stride length.

However, when playing on a course for the first time, due to unfamiliarity, it is common for a mistake in judging the situation by one or two strokes to result in a series of strokes and ruin your score, so you must play with cool-headed judgment and self-control.

Therefore, Gary Player emphasized that the three major requirements for a golfer are not only technique, but also mental strength and basic physical strength.

It is true that golfers go to practice ranges and continuously study to improve their skills, but they often do not pay special attention to mental strength and basic physical strength training.

By doing so, you will feel rewarded when your skills improve and your score improves. And as you get older, won't you become more proud of yourself as a golfer if you settle into better sports?

B. People called 'single'

When you go to a golf course, as soon as you enter any country club, there is a board with the member's name and handicap written on it.

Among them, what stands out most are the so-called single-digit handicap players with a handicap of 1 to 9. Among them, there are very few people with a handicap of 1, 2, or 3, and even if there are, there are only one or two players, and the number of players with a handicap of 9 or less is extremely limited, so there are only less than 10 players.

And a significant number of players are in the so-called 80s, with handicaps of 10, 12, 15, and 18, and most of the rest are so densely filled that it is difficult to even find their names in the handicap 19 or higher column. There are also members who are not on the list.

The number of members is not constant depending on the club, but based on about 1,000 people per 18 holes, about 1%, and even with 1,800 people, about 0.6% of people can be said to be so-called single handicappers.

Considering that about one person in every 100 people hits their 70s, this is a rather generous figure. However, in a friendly match between friends, if someone hits 70, we treat them generously by labeling them as 'single'.

Even so, it is not easy to become one of 100 or 180 single people, and it is a position that can only be achieved by accumulating considerable skills and experience. There are quite a few professionals who hit over 80 during competition.

Even if you hit a tee shot from a regular tee, your driver shot must be over 230 yards to hit the 70s, and it is not very common for golfers to actually hit longer than that.

Unless you are a player who uses an iron to hit the green with a second shot in the middle course or get on the edge and then compete with a putter, hitting 70s is impossible for a weekend golfer.

Therefore, no matter how gifted these single handicappers are, can we say that they are gurus who have temporarily become crazy about golf and have mastered the Tao?

Excluding these golfers who have invested money, time, and passion to experience the essence of golf, the majority of amateur golfers are in the middle of playing well even into their 80s, and by the time they break 90 and hit 80, it would be nice to buy a round of golf for their friends.

Therefore, except for those who are natural long hitters or those who have practiced a lot and can reach quite a distance, on average, no matter how much they hit from regular tees, it is difficult to hit in the 70s and shouldn't they be satisfied with the 80s?

Rather, even if you are in your 80s, it would be much better to use polite manners, etiquette, and good sense to use this long-awaited opportunity as a means of relieving stress during the week.

However, this does not mean that you should not hit the 70s. As the fun of being a golfer is to constantly improve your skills and reduce your score by even one bit, you should not neglect your efforts for self-improvement as you can reduce your score by improving your short game or improving your putting if you do not reach the distance.

However, even if you hit 70 once in a while, maintaining it is not easy. It is difficult for an amateur golfer who does not play golf as a profession but as a pastime to maintain his average age in his 70s. In order to do this, you must increase the number of times and opportunities to go to the golf course and go to the practice range to constantly improve your skills.

How many people actually have that much time, energy, and leisure? Is it 1% or 0.6%?

C. The road to 'single'

The best thing about being an amateur golfer is, of course, being single. No matter how much fun you play, golf is not fun unless your score decreases as your skills improve. Moreover, if you are young, you play golf for the fun of lowering your score by getting to the pin while hitting the pin as much distance as others, but even if you have a lot of money and can afford it, if your score does not improve at all, you will gradually lose interest in golf.

However, in most cases, when playing golf, as time goes by and the number of times you go out to the field increases, you gradually get the hang of it and your score decreases. Not only can you never put down a golf club once you pick it up, but you also have to look through books and videos to improve your skills. It is **a general tendency to strive** for.

However, the majority of amateur golfers are average golfers who break 90 and hit the 80s, but sometimes hit the 90s again and go back and forth in the 90s. Breaking 85, then 80, and hitting 70 normally seem like a long shot for middle-aged golfers who started playing at an older age. It is probably no coincidence that people say that if you start at age 30, you can hit a handicap of 15, and if you start at age 40, you can reach a handiness of 20.

However, even if you are a golfer who started in middle age, the problem is different if you have strengthened your body through other exercises before. In most cases, office workers who regularly play sports at work, such as tennis, baseball, or billiards, as a hobby, or people who retired from sports and play golf have excellent motor skills, and their scores usually improve as their skills rapidly improve.

However, due to the unique characteristics of golf, even if they hit long shots, it is not easy to break the 90s, go through the mid-80s, and hit the 70s. It is the habit of amateur golfers to hit 78-79 once, but then hit 80 again and go straight to the practice range again.

In fact, there are many cases where even professional golfers who play golf and make a living from it hit over 80 when they are not hitting well. Moreover, they are amateurs.

Nevertheless, enthusiasts who have friends who are good at golf or who are into golf and feel like they will become single if they do well will make every effort to hit 70 by any means possible.

Moreover, if I go to a friendly golf tournament and come in first or second place, I look through books and videos on golf and do my best to find the secrets of long shots, approaches, and putting in order to improve my skills with the goal of becoming a medalist.

Therefore, the road to singleness is a difficult and lonely road. In order to become one of the singles, which accounts for less than 1–2% of all golfers, you must have a strong mentality, consistent physical training, and constantly hone your skills. Moreover, it is difficult to consistently stay in your 70s without going through a training process comparable to that of a professional.

Therefore, an amateur golfer who enjoys leisure time may be forced to choose between a career and a professional golfer if he wants to go solo. The road to singleness is a lonely and difficult road. And it is the road to the top that one day we must come down.

D. The world of golf and competition

No matter what sport, there is bound to be competition. The winner experiences the joy of ecstasy, while the loser cannot help but feel bitterness and regret and vows to make a comeback.

In all sports, there is no permanent winner, so even a winner may be pushed out by the previous loser in the next match without hard work and rigorous training. And the new winner who succeeds again clenches his fists and enjoys the joy of becoming a new prince.

The same goes for the world of golf. In major competitions that take place every year, a new champion is born and yesterday's winner takes a knee and the leading role changes.

Jack Nicklaus, Greg Norman, Nick Faldo, Nick Price, Fred Couples, and Davis Love III, who once dominated the world, have faded with the emergence of new powerhouses, and in recent years, they have been replaced by new rookies. there is. It feels like the Spring and Autumn Warring States Period is unfolding, and attention is focused on who will unify the world in the future.

Spectators who watch the fierce competition taking place in the professional world also become excited as they watch their favorite players win or lose.

Compared to professionals, there is no world of fierce competition for amateur golfers. However, amateurs experience the inner pleasure of winning by fighting against themselves as amateurs, challenging themselves and challenging their scores. And by demonstrating their skills at fraternity, alumni, and workplace competitions, they sometimes end up winning trophies, and sometimes they end up winning long-distance awards, near-list awards, and luck awards.

While the competitive world of professional golf is cold, the world of amateur golf enlivens the social atmosphere with joy, relaxation, topics, rumors, status, and social interaction.

While professional golfers use golf as a means of making a living, and winning and losing become a measure of life and death, amateur golfers have a separate means of making a living and choose golf among various leisure sports to enjoy their leisure time, thus suffering from the same miserable results and losses as professionals. Rather than becoming obsessed, more emphasis is placed on making good use of social leisure through golf.

However, golf is a competitive game, so once you have a certain level of skill, you can test your skills by participating in the club championship competition at your club or in the amateur championship competition to show off your skills to the fullest.

In particular, there are many cases where young junior golfers who have not yet made a living challenge themselves to various competitions in order to seek advancement into the professional ranks. In these cases, they are far from average golfers like us.

And in order to experience the thrill of winning, some people bet with money, causing social controversy.

All games and sports have certain rules, and if you deviate from them, you will already lose their character as a game or sport and become the target of criticism, and you must refrain from such actions to protect the purity of golf.

Therefore, in order to foster golf as a healthy sport and encourage interest as a game, it is most important for each person to stick to the rules of golf, improve their skills, and use it as an opportunity for self-development.

E. The joy of a senior golfer

Senior golfers over the age of 50 not only have lower physical strength and worse eyesight than regular golfers, but also sometimes suffer from illness, so they have to play golf with various handicaps.

In the United States, he plays on the regular tour, but when he turns 50, he participates in a separate senior tour and has another fun experience.

The U. S. Senior Tour determines the winner by reducing one round to three rounds, and the atmosphere is softer than the regular tour, and the faces of the participants do not change much.

The Senior Tour, which initially grew rapidly around Arnold Palmer, included Bob Charles, Lee Trevino, Jim Colbert, Jack Nicklaus, and Chi Chi Rodriguez. Former champions such as Chi Rodriguez and new champions such as Raymond Floyd and Hale Irwin were coming together to form a field of victory and harmony.

As people get older, it is inevitable that not only will their physical stamina decline compared to when they were younger, but their eyesight also decline, which undermine the basic conditions necessary for golf.

However, as they free themselves from the burden of their children's education, become socially established, and have the financial resources and time to spare, they enter an age where they can enjoy leisure time by playing golf in earnest.

In Korea, golf began to be popularized only recently, and because life was difficult in the past, there are only a few older golfers who started early, and most amateur golfers belong to the younger age group.

However, since golf is a sport that can be enjoyed throughout one's life, anyone who gets into it will sooner or later become a senior golfer. And although the distance is lower than that of younger people, they can cover the field with an experienced game and stable swing.

In particular, you can experience the essence of golf by demonstrating outstanding skills in close approach shots, short games around the green, and handling putts on the green.

For amateur golfers, this is the golden age when they can enjoy golf leisurely, and recently, some people have picked up golf as a hobby and picked up a golf club at a young age.

However, the reality in our country is that once you enter your 60s, your physical strength declines rapidly and some of your friends have passed away, so the number of people who continue to play golf is decreasing, and its existence is gradually fading away in favor of the younger generation.

Compared to other countries, seniors dominate golf courses due to the development of a thorough social security system and low prices. Considering the fact that our country has a small land mass and the golfing population is rapidly increasing due to the recent rapid improvement in living standards, it is understandable that a large number of young people are taking over golf courses.

As they soon become senior golfers and follow in their parents' footsteps, the level of senior golfers in our country will improve significantly, and as they age into their 60s and 70s, there will be age shooters who score lower than their age. You will reach the pinnacle of your golf career, showing off your health and skills, and experience the joy of a new life.

And as I coach my younger generation and my children, I look forward to seeing world-dominant golfers emerge from our country as well, and begin a new life in golf.

12. Manner and Etiquette in Golf

The birthplace of golf, the oldest and most traditional place, St. Andrews in Scotland. The golf club R&A was founded here in 1754. The law created here became the international law of golf that must be observed everywhere in the world.

It is the oldest and most widely observed autonomous law. Whether you go east, west, south, or north, it was all the same articles of law. Thereafter, as the world changed, the rules of golf also changed, and the American golf association USGA joined in 1894. Now, these two organizations, S&A and the USGA, are working together to modernize the rules of golf. Two and a half centuries passed thereafter, golf has prospered, the rules have been simplified, and everyone is accepted and treated equally, and it is expected that it will continue to modernize and develop further in the future.

Now in the 21st century. people from almost all over the world are playing golf together, all races are joining in play and so it can be said that a symbol of world peace is blossoming here.

So it has become an eternal law of the world and now everybody want to read it at least once and go out into the field and become a gentleman and a lady like everyone else.

Even if you haven't read the Six Laws of the country, you must read and practice this regulations and use them not only in the UK and the USA, but also when you go to Thailand and New Zealand and anywhere else. I haven't known yet so comfortable and so mysterious it is.

A. You should Know
the rules of golf

The followings are some of the questions asked by the Korea Women's Golf Association about the golf rules for aspiring professionals in the spring of 1996.

1. Can you remove the pine cones next to the ball in the bunker? What if there are cigarette butts?

2. Is the ball caught on the OB line an OB ball or not?

3. What should you do if the ball is caught in the rubber trap on the bunker hill and the ball moves while you are clearing the trap?

4. What should you do if the ball moves without being hit after addressing from a place other than the teeing ground?

5. If the ball comes to rest on a cigarette butt on the through green, can you hit it after removing the cigarette butt?

What percentage of our amateur golfers actually know and play these actual golf rules? Of course, you probably knew the basic rules, such as the person who hit well on the previous hole takes the honor and hits the ball in the order of precedence, or on the green, the person who is farthest from the hole cup on the green must hit first, or a mishit ball must be found and hit within 3 minutes, but how many amateur golfers play golf after learning the full text of the golf rules and supplements, starting with Chapter 1, Etiquette?

In fact, isn't it true that most amateur golfers go out into the field and enjoy golf, knowing only part of the rules they heard fragmentarily from their friends, even though they don't know the details of the rules?

However, when it comes to selecting a club champion or participating in professional and amateur (Pro—Am) competitions, won't you be embarrassed if you participate without knowing the rules?

As golf has rapidly become more popular, it has become common to see things that go against manners, such as casually stepping on someone else's putt line on the green, or moving to the other side of the line without moving out of the way when trying to putt, or making noise.

Since no game can be established without rules, and golf is a game that involves self-management, there have been reports of unfortunate events, such as even pros being disqualified for failing to sign score cards or hitting provisional balls without clear communication to the opponent, has happened many times over the past years.

Also, if pine cones in a bunker cannot be removed because they are natural obstacles, and cigarette butts can be removed because they are artificial obstacles, can stone mixed in the sand be removed or not?

In the 1996 Women's Rose Open held at 88CC, was the decision made on the question raised by Carrie Webb, number one in money rankings, about whether it was okay to remove a stone from the 16th hole, good or bad?

When applying golf rules in practice, it is not

always easy to strictly apply them depending on the numerous situations and cases.

But the rules of golf aren't just there to impose penalties. The ball that entered the mole hole can be dropped within 1 club length, or in casual water such as puddles formed on a rainy day or snow and ice in winter, it can be dropped within 1 club length, or even when tree supports are in the way. There are cases where the play can be advantageous, such as being able to drop and hit within 1 club length. Therefore, if you know the rules of golf, you can play at an advantage.

The Rules of Golf, which are almost universally common, have become the standard for golf games, and since a game cannot be played without following the rules, it would be wise to know the minimum rules before playing in practice. Since golf is a sport that requires mental and technical skills that are close to law, if you play while knowing the rules that must be followed, it adds to the fun and becomes a means of self-training, further arousing interest. Moreover, recently, the golf rules were greatly relaxed in 2019 and again in 2023, reforming them to suit the current times, making golf more accessible to the general public, now, let's read the recently revised golf rules.

B. Manner and etiquette

The score in golf is determined by the number of strokes, but not necessarily solely by the number of strokes. Golf rules provide for strict penalty points for various cases that violate manners and etiquette, and in cases of bad manners, such as intentionally committing a serious foul, a severe penalty of disqualification from the game is given.

In other words, before the recent rule revision, cheating the score, continuing to play the wrong ball, intentionally moving the ball, incorrectly writing the score card, or failing to sign were punishable by a severe penalty of disqualification from the game. A violation of the rules one level lower than this is subject to a 2-stroke penalty, and OB due to bad luck and inexperience, lost balls, etc. were subject to a one-stroke penalty

In other words, it placed importance not only on the number of strokes but also the player's personality and mental aspect, and imposes penalty points when it causes discomfort to others or interferes with strict play, thereby requiring gentlemanly ethics.

Recently, the popularity of golf has rapidly progressed everywhere, and as golf has spread worldwide, some of the morals of golf have been broken and become a little bit vulgarized and compliance with the rules of golf has become lax, often leading to trouble.

In fact, the rules of golf are too complicated for an amateur golfer to know and follow every details of the rules of golf, and not only does it take time to understand each and every one of these rules, but it is also said that applying strict rules reduce the entertainment factor for average golfers, so in cases where it is not a match, there wee often cases where they proceed as conveniently as possible such as giving a mulligan or so-called give.

However, fundamentally, the true essence of golf can only be felt when it is played according to the rules based on manners and etiquette, so it is a game of friendly competition between players by playing a game that does not significantly deviate from the basic spirit of golf. How do you think this would add to the enjoyment of golf ?

Nevertheless, there were cases where problems arose due to the lack of proficiency in the rules of golf not only among amateur golfers but also among aspiring pros and professional golfers. Therefore, in order to improve the quality of golf in the future, we need to educate ourselves on the rules of golf and encourage their compliance to the need to spread it.

As golf is a sport that is widely spread internationally, it can be said that manners and etiquette are more desperately needed than scores, especially when going abroad and playing social golf with foreigners. Taking these factors into consideration, S&A and the USGA have also joined forces to significantly revise the golf rules to modernize and simplify golf rules starting from 2019.

While playing 18 holes, you can get to know the other golfer's personality and characters, and golf allows you to expose your own personality and character to the other golfers.

Moreover, as the number of Koreans advancing to the international stage is rapidly increasing recently, manners and compliance with etiquette are not just an individual's problem, but also leap forward to become a manner issue for all golfers in the world, by making it an issue that we all need to reflect on it.

In that sense, we hope that we will not forget that it is the important duty of the general public to learn the rules of golf as time allows and to enjoy golf while adapting to social morals and culture as well as the rules of golf.

C. Etiquette on the green

There are few sports that require manners and etiquette like golf. At first glance, etiquette in the teeing area as well as various requirements until the hole is out may seem to be required as simple and gentlemanly, but failing to do so can have a significant impact directly or indirectly on play and scores.

Among them, the most strictly required and observed etiquette are manners and etiquette on the putting green.

Usually, until you get on the green, all actions are mainly done with a swing movement centered on the distance, but once you get on the green, you are not different from a fighter on a stage competing with one goal in front of you.

Therefore, putting on the green, which is the final blow while under the spotlight of fellow competitors, is comparable to a matador's strike and requires mental concentration like an archer pulling an arrow string.

In order to smoothly putt in such a state of extreme mental tension, chatting while putting is prohibited, as well as any movement of objects that come into the field of view of the putting golfer is also not allowed. as stipulated in Chapter 1 of the Golf Rules, Etiquette.

The act of trying to cup in a hole requires extreme nerve tension and mental concentration, much more than a tee shot, bunker shot, or fairway shot. That's why they say that some golfers fall down on the green in their old age.

Despite the requirement for such etiquette, in reality, the problem for amateur golfers is that, depending on the person, there is sometimes small talk, spike marks, and crossing of the line before and after putting.

Even if people don't say a word, if people cross the line or move from where they are trying to putt, the putter's concentration is disrupted and the ball misses the cup and goes over or sideways.

For low handicappers who are competing for a point or two, mistakes like this are more critical, and it will not be once or twice that they ruin their next shot or cut off their earned score.

In times like these, experts recommend that you do not attempt putting, but rather turn your body around completely, catch your breath, and then return to the putting position.

The biggest reason for making a mistake in putting is being unable to accurately read the state of the green and not concentrating and failing to enjoy the feeling of putting. That is why you must calm your emotions, calm your mind and putt as if you were putting the ball into a quiet lake.

Just as baduk(Oriental Chess Game) you can be ruined by one misplaced move, a single mistake in golf on the green can continue to affect the next hole and result in ruining a good play. Golf is really something you don't even know about.

D. touch play

The ball must be played as it is, except in special cases. Therefore, the so-called touch play, which involves moving the ball to a place with a good lie, is illegal, and in principle, a penalty point is added.   When professionals compete, this rule applies and they must never do touch play, but touch play among amateur golfers in Korea has almost become a trend.

There seems to be several reasons for this. In situations like Korea, where it is difficult to maintain golf course grass due to the clear seasonal fluctuations between spring, summer, and fall, the grass is uneven and difficult to play on, and there are local rules that require tee play in winter. The reality is that we cannot uniformly criticize touch play.

However, except in unavoidable cases approved by local rules, it is necessary to reconsider the habit of playing touch play on days with good grass management and sunny weather, such as those recently built at new golf courses.

"Touch play" has begun to spread as entertainment golf was once popular and these days there are beginners who are unfamiliar with the rules. It is in fact a devil's temptation for ordinary players who want to enjoy golf as a sport.

However, it is like picking up a ball in the rough or coming out of a bunker and hitting it, so it is not a game from the beginning.

'As it is' In some ways, it can be said to be an expression of the desire to abandon the pure joy of golf, which is a bold challenge by overcoming a given situation like fate, to pursue only easy results.

There was once a shameless player who twisted the grass from the fairway to make a temporary tee, but this can be said to be an ignorant act that insults golf.

Moreover, for average golfers who want to train their mind and body through golf and enjoy it as a sport, touch play can be said to be an act of self-deception that hinders the improvement of golf skills.

The ball must be struck differently depending on the lie condition, and the distance and trajectory change.

Therefore, in the process of devising a suitable batting method, new skills are learned and contributed to improving the score, but touch play deprives oneself of such opportunities and instills a mentality to escape the occasional crisis, which has a negative effect on personality formation.

Recently, many people have been going abroad and playing with foreigners, but it is this touch play that is problematic. I think it is time for our players, who do not hesitate to break the rules, to reflect on their actions.

At one business group, there was a golf boom and people were bragging about how good they were at playing. And so the group opened the competition and strictly applied the rules and played with no touch and no give. As a result, only one person broke 100, and that was 98. You can see how inaccurate our handy is.

Therefore, wouldn't it be fun to develop your skills and train your mind and body by strictly adhering to no touch play?

13. The Rules of St. Andrews

In the birthplace of golf, the oldest and most traditional place, St. Andrews, Scotland. The golf club R&A was founded in 1754. The law created there became the international law of golf that must be observed by golfers everywhere in the world. It is the oldest and most widely observed autonomous law. Whether you go east, west, south, or north, it was all the same 34 articles of law.

Afterwards, as the world changed, the rules of golf also changed and the American golf association USGA joined in 1894. Now, these two organizations, S&A and the USGA, are working together to modernize the rules of golf. Two and a half centuries later, the golf has prospered and the rules have been simplified and everyone is accepted and treated equally and it is expected that it will continue to modernize and develop further in the future.

In another words, people from almost all over the world began playing golf, people of all races joined in together and now it could be said that a world symbol of peace was blossoming here

So it has become an eternal law of the world and now everyone want to read it at least once and go out into the field and become a lady and gentleman like everyone else. Even if you haven't read the Six Laws, you can read and practice this rules and use it not only in the UK and the US, but also when you go to Thailand and New Zealand and anywhere else. It is so comfortable and so mysterious everywhere.

A. The basic golf rules and their revision

By a brief look at the history of golf rules we can divide it into 5 stages. From 1744 to 1899, the first 13 rules of golf were established during the period of golf's settlement. Then In 1894, the USGA was founded. And 1899-1934 was a period of revision and interpretation of the rules, during which a re-established rule book was published. During the period 1934-1952 recognizing the need for unified golf rules, the R&A and USGA each established and applied golf rules. The pursuit of uniformity continued from 1952 to 1984, with the first unified rules adopted in 1952, and as of 1984, changes in the rules of golf over the past 300 years have demonstrated the continued need for definition, clarity, and revision.

The basic considerations are at the heart of current rule modernization initiatives but it can be said that it is driving change more, and the goal could be said to be a process of rule revision to create up-to-date rules that meet the needs of games played around the world.

In the future too, golf will continue to expand into new places and the number of new golfers will increase, and the game that continues to move forward with the emergence of challenging new technologies will require modern and more useful measures, so the R&A and USGA will continue to address all of these tasks, and continue to provide leadership and guidance.

The USGA announced a summary of seven things it considers big changes. Including several changes to existing rules, and so the total number of rules was reduced from 34 rules to 24. To alleviate and eliminate penalties related to "moving balls," there will no longer be penalties for balls accidentally moved on the putting green or for balls moved during a ball search. And a player is no longer liable for a moved ball unless it is "virtually certain" that he or she moved the ball.

1) Relaxation of putting green rules.

There was no penalty for hitting the flagstick on the putting green of a hole by playing toward an unattended flagpole. This means that a player may putt without removing the flagstick or without attending to it. However now players will be able to repair spike marks, any damage to the green caused by golf shoes, animals, or other damage. And there was no penalty for touching the putting line. A ball that is marked, lifted, and replaced on the putting green can be replaced to its original position and played even if the ball moves.

2) Easing of "Penalty areas".

In the Vault area, which was called a water hazard until now, in the future, not only areas with water, but the red or yellow penalty area(Penalty stroke area) can also include deserts, deep forests, and volcanic rock areas. The use of the red penalty area where parallel relief is possible has been expanded, and there is no penalty for moving or touching the loose impediment within the penalty area, and there is no penalty for touching the ground or water within the penalty area. Among the relief options for a ball that enters the red penalty area, there is no longer an option to drop it at an alternative spot on the other side.

3) Relaxation of bunker rules

There is no penalty for moving loose impediments in the bunker, and there is no penalty for generally touching the sand with your hand or club. Some restrictions (e. g. touching the club to the ground next to the ball) were decided to keep because they made playing in the sand challenging. When a ball is declared unplayable inside a bunker, a penalty of 2 strokes is imposed and an option to play from outside the bunker has been added.

However, although it has been alleviated, the sand in the bunker cannot be touched as follows. Testing the condition of bunkers, hitting the front or back of the ball with a club, or touching the sand during practice swings or backswings is not permitted.

Trusting the player's truthfulness, the decision was made to support the player's "reasonable judgment" when measuring or measuring a place, line, area or distance, even if a video review later reveals that the decision was incorrect. There is no longer a need to notify fellow players in advance when lifting a ball to check if it is one's own or to check for damage. It can be said that this amendment provided very high level of behavior guidelines to all players to support speed of play. and also reduced the time to find a lost item from 5 minutes to 3 minutes. In stroke competitions, "Ready Golf" was positively encouraged with players ready to play playing first, and players were encouraged not to spend more than 40 seconds making a stroke, and to take other measures to increase the speed of play.

To simplify the relief process, a new relief process has been established such as where the ball is dropped, placed in play, and played from a specific relief location, AMD allowing the ball to be dropped directly over the ground, any growing grass, or other object on the ground, thereby reducing the drop procedures.

And when dropping the ball, the ball can be dropped from a low height of at least 1 inch, almost on the ground.

In addition, the committee can set and implement a maximum score for each hole, and if more strokes are recorded than the set score, the hole can no longer be played and must be moved to the next hole.

As mentioned above, the USGA made a summary announcement, but in order to understand the above content a little better, it is necessary to understand the definition of terms, which is one of the most important things.

B. The recent Revision of golf rules

1) Rules coming into force in 2019

The golf rules, which came into effect from January 2019, are the product of a plan to modernize the rules led by members of the R&A and USGA rules committees, and are the result of reflecting the diverse opinions of numerous golfers around the world. This revision has been fundamental and extensive to ensure that the core principles and characteristics of golf are maintained, while taking into account the needs of all golfers and making it easier for anyone to understand and apply the rules. As a result, the revised rules are more consistent, simpler, and fairer compared to the past rules.

The rules of golf should be easily understandable to everyone and provide clear answers to the problems that arise when golfers of different abilities play on different types of courses around the world. Those who wish to learn more about referees, committees and rules can find "Rules of Golf" in print or digital versions.

In addition, a new "Official Guide to the Rules of Golf" containing "Committee Procedures" and "Interpretation of the Rules of Golf" containing recommendations on how to conduct general play and competitions has been prepared to ensure that these modernized rules are fairer and effective. Mark Reinman, chairman of the USGA Rules Committee, said he believes it will ensure that it is not only less complex and easier to understand, but also better suited to the issues facing golf, such as increasing the speed of play and environmental stewardship.

2) Five rules of golf revised for 2023

As the golf population is rapidly increasing and many people around the world are enjoying golf, S&A and the USGA have joined forces to embrace all these people, further popularize golf in the future and educate the public on golf. Through the new rule revision, the golf rules have been revised as follows to make it easier and more convenient to play golf. The important points are summarized as follows.

a) When the golf ball is in the perfect position to hit, the golfer desperately hopes that the ball will not move. However, there are times when a situation arises in which the ball moves unintentionally. Previously, if the ball moved, you had to hit the shot from where it moved, and if it went into a penalty area such as a hazard or OB, you had to take a penalty and play again.

However, after the rule was revised, if the ball moved alone, the ball can be moved to its original location, and if the ball moves due to natural forces, it can be played without penalty.

b) Next, the penalty for filling out the score card incorrectly has been relaxed. A golf game is played with four people on a team. Each player writes down the score of the game and submits the score after the game is over, and if you did not sign your score card, your score would not be recognized and you would be immediately disqualified.

However, thanks to a revision to the golf rules, players will no longer be disqualified if there is no signature on the score card. Also, if the handicap was not written down or written incorrectly after the game, a penalty was imposed in the past, but now everything has been digitalized and then the responsibility has been revised to place responsibility on the organizer rather than the golfer.

c) While playing a golf game, a golf club may suddenly broke or damaged the game. And golfers have difficulty progressing the game and face embarrassing moments. And If the driver is damaged during the game, you will have to tee off with a wood. In this case, it is difficult to achieve a better record than the original score, and if this happens in an important game, a situation may arise where the game itself has to be abandoned.

Many golfers were having difficulties due to club damage that occurred during the game, but the revised rules in 2023 now allow for replacement and repair of golf clubs damaged during the golf play. Of course, even though the rules have been revised like this, it does not apply to cases where the club is intentionally damaged.

d) The rear line relief rules have also been relaxed. In a situation where relief is provided to the back line in the existing penalty area, dropping the ball close to the pin from the reference point was not recognized. If you dropped it too close, you might have to drop it again. Now, if the ball stops within one club distance after a back line relief drop, you can continue play without dropping it again.

e) Lastly, the rules for golfers with disabilities have been improved. Before the revision, separate rules were set for golfers with disabilities according to the organizing committee. For example, if the local rules stipulate that players cannot be accompanied by a helper, a situation may arise where they face difficulties because they cannot play the game without a helper.

From January 2023, official golf rules, rather than separate rules set by the organizers, will apply to all competitions. With this revised rule, disabled golfers no longer need to check whether there is a local rule for accompanying a helper at every competition, but now can be accompanied by a helper at every match.

These revised rules have made it possible to play the game more fairly than ever before. If you look at past professional matches, there were many cases where the rankings of the players were divided by just one stroke. It is expected that the revised golf rules will reduce the number of professional players who unfairly lose their scores due to penalty strokes.

In the case of amateur golfers who enjoy golf as a hobby, they may not play by perfectly applying all the changed rules during their rounds, but it will still be of great help to be aware of the changed rules.

14. Tripitaka Koreana

The Goryeo Tripitaka Koreana, which contains 84,000 teachings of the Buddha. Magnificent scale, extensive content were completed in spite of rain or shine, it took 16 years to complete. An unprecedented national treasure.

Even if no one told you to play golf, once you get into it, you cannot let it go, no matter whether it rains or snows, 12 months a year, 365 days a year. That sincerity and perseverance are enough to build a large castle and a long embankment. Regardless of age or gender, multiple generations come together as one, tens of thousands of people gather in the field for golf, and the manpower is more than enough to build a pyramid or block the Nile River. The Great Wall of China wasn't built in just one or two days.

A. Going to play Golf early in the morning without good sleeping.

Even if you wake up at 3 a.m. and try to go back to sleep, it's too late to make it to the 6:06 tee time, so everyone has probably had the experience of leaving home at 4:30 with their eyes wide open and having trouble sleeping.

Moreover, due to the booking difficulties these days, there are times when you can't even think of going to a nearby golf course and so you have to drive more than two hours away, so where can you get a good night's sleep? It can be said that the golf war already begins here. Not only that, when you think about how you came home early from a drinking party last night and was cautious about getting in and out of the house out of fear of disturbing your child's studies, golf is something that makes you anxious to play well this time.

Not only that, you left home early mooning carrying the map book you had read yesterday out of fear of getting lost and not being able to find the new golf course, which you are visiting for the first time. But isn't it inevitable to feel anxious?

In most cases, when you arrive at the clubhouse and collect your golf equipment, you will often find that you have left out your hat or socks, or that you have not brought a change of shirt, or that you have also left out your windbreaker or umbrella.

However, you can't go home again, and since the clubhouse concession stand isn't open yet, you can't get it, so you have no choice but to move to the first hole. With your face frazzled and still half-asleep, you draw a lot and hit your first tee shot. Your body is heavy and you have no sense of control, so the ball you hit with your driver curves to the right and falls into the rough.

Before starting any exercise, you need to properly warm up and develop a sense of movement before actually practicing it, but since you stood on the teeing area without even having time to warm up, there was no way you could hit it properly. Of course, it's not just you, it's the same for everyone you play with.

But today seems a little better than last week. Last time, there was a thick fog and you had a hard time finding the ball because you didn't know where it flew, but today Yoon can still see the ball, so I guess it's a good thing for you.

You still found the ball in the rough easily, but there was a tree in front of you your blocking your path, so you had no choice but to pull it out to the fairway, so you hit it with a 5-iron, but it stopped at most 100 meters in front, so there was still 180 meters left to the green, so you took out the spoon.

However, there was no way the ball would hit the green, and it would inevitably end up in a bunker. Even if your tried a bunker shot from the bunker and got the ball out, it was too far to make a one-putt, so you finished with a two-putt, but when you counted all shots, it was a double bogey.

Since you doubled from the first hole, you don't feel very good, and since your body is still not warmed up, there is no way you can get it right on the second or third hole, so your score starts to miss. you decided to lower your score for a long time ago, but you forgot about it before you knew it and remembered it only on the fourth hole, so when will you make up for it?

You can't stop your greed, so you grab the driver and hit it with all your might, but the ball still bends and flies away, so you can't even dream of making a par or a birdie. The dew on the green is due to the footprints of several people, so you don't know with how much sense you should hit the ball, so the distance from the first hole is always short. This time, you hit a little harder and overshot the hole and hit a downhill putt, which only made you even more anxious

However, as the sun, which had been rising in the eastern sky far away, now rises in the sky and shines its rays, your mind feels refreshed and your body seems to relax, and from then on, you begin to feel better little by little. In particular, as early morning golf has become more frequent in recent years, this is an inevitable phenomenon due to the expansion of the golf population and the worsening booking difficulties.

Then, you wonder to yourself who is going to tee it up at the golden hour of 9 or 10, and when you think about the fight you had all morning on Tuesday with your phone in hand, you end up masturbating and thinking that you should play golf like this at least.

So, when you pull yourself together, play carefully, and finish the 9 out course in the first half, you still hit 45, so you end up with a bogey play. As you enter the course in the second half, your body will relax, the dew will soon disappear on the green, and the ball will hit faster, so if you don't putt more carefully than before, you will usually end up overshooting the hole.

However, you can avoid double and triple bogeys, catch waves sometimes, and sometimes catch birdies. The second half score is a few points lower than the first half, and you manage to finish within 90, hitting one or two points more than your handicap. Is this the best score on days when you had trouble sleeping in the morning? It was just like that last time too.

B. Play in the rain
in the afternoon

At some point in our country, golf was recognized as a sport that could be played at any time regardless of the weather. Whether it was raining or snowing, and even if in the hot summer rain continued to fall or in winter the field was covered in white snow, people played golf diligently as long as the golf club did not close the course.

It is said that there are two main reasons why there are golf clubs with unique charm. First of all, golf is a business aimed at generating income, so it is open regardless of the weather and allows a large number of people, and the other is on the player side. how are you doing?

Even if you can play today or tomorrow, even if you are managing the back of a few weeks or a severe month, there is a greater meaning in having an outdoor place to chat with your lizard pet for a long time due to the environment not being able to play. Being unaffected by the weather also has social significance.

The problem is that, unlike normal play, such plays in the rain do not go well and often result in misses, resulting in poor scores, which usually results in long-awaited opportunities and dreams being dashed.

Usually, when playing in the rain, even if you wear a raincoat, it is cumbersome and the rain cannot be completely blocked, so your swing is hindered, so the distance you usually hit is significantly lower than your usual distance.

In addition, sometimes there is fog, making it difficult to determine direction and distance, and you often end up in a bunker or rough.

It is common for grips with wet hands to cause your hands to slip and not be able to hold the club properly, resulting in limited distance and twisted direction.

Is that it? Because I have to carry an umbrella unlike usual, my grip sense becomes dull, and when I ride a cart like these days, I have to carry a couple of clubs, so my sense of grip becomes dull even more.

Nevertheless, amateur golfers try to cover the distance as usual when the weather is good, swinging the driver and pulling out the fairway wood to aim directly for the pin.

Even though the situation has changed, I still swing the same way I did on a nice day, so there's no way I can hit it right, right? Therefore, when playing in the rain, it is necessary to readjust your goals for the day.

You must assume a play that is different from your usual play, such as aiming for a bogey play rather than par, preventing missed shots by placing more importance on direction than distance, or making shots that avoid bunkers as much as possible.

In that respect, for tee shots, you can use a spoon, baffy, or cleek rather than a driver, and in my experience, using an iron rather than a wood, especially on the fairway, has a higher hit rate.

However, the biggest problem with playing in the rain is that the grip is slippery, so to prevent this, you should prepare three or four gloves in advance and a towel to wipe the grip area. You should also prepare extra socks.

No matter how strong a person's grip is, they cannot properly handle a wet grip, so in most cases, the ball flies to the right. In that regard, one way is to aim to the left, taking into account the inevitable slipping when playing with a wet glove.

Anyway, playing in the rain on a rainy day is difficult. If you play with that in mind, you'll be calm, but if you don't and try to hit as usual, you'll end up with frustrating shots. It's also a day where you have to be careful when playing.

C. Winter Golf

Golf can be said to be a sport enjoyed in spring, summer, and fall when the weather is nice. Important matches, both internationally and domestically, are usually held during this period, and it can be said that it is unsuitable to play golf in the cold winter.

However, due to our country's special climatic conditions and limited land in our country where it is difficult for golfers to find other suitable places in the winter, golf has no choice but to continue to be played even in the winter.

However, in winter, not only is the weather cold, but it also snows and the grass is frozen or covered with snow, making it virtually impossible to play normally. Not only does the player's body shrink, their hands get cold, their grip is poor, and their swing becomes unbalanced. I am having a hard time not being able to catch it.

Nevertheless, since you cannot predict the weather in advance and cannot miss a long-awaited opportunity in the midst of a booking crisis, you usually continue playing as is.

As a result, in winter, players usually wear underwear, winter clothing, or gloves on both hands, which makes their body more sluggish and does not provide proper feel, making it difficult to control the ball and resulting in poor scores.

However, these days do not last all winter, and sometimes there are warm sunny days to warm up your body.

Recently, with the development of clothing materials, thin winter clothing and cold weather gear have also been released to help with play.

However, it is not a fundamental solution, so some people go on expeditions to warm southern countries or take a break for a while.

The problem with winter golf is that the weather is cold and the grass freezes, causing a lot of balls to bounce. So, the ball after a tee shot rolls endlessly and goes to the wrong place, or it is difficult to place the ball on the intended spot during the approach, and backspin is difficult.

Meanwhile, on the grass on the green, the ball does not roll straight and changes direction in the morning due to frost. During the day, there is a difference between a shaded area and a sunny area, causing the cheeks to bounce.

Therefore, some golf courses require tee play in the winter, and even iron shots have to be played from the tee, forcing Koreans to practice their winter golf skills.

I think the reason Korean professional golfers are weak at international competitions is because it is difficult to practice in the winter and their rhythm is broken.

In the winter, you will need to maintain your stamina more than your score and continue playing without losing your sense of rhythm to prepare for full-scale play in the spring.

Therefore, some golf courses require tee play in the winter, and even iron shots have to be played from the tee, forcing Koreans to practice their winter golf skills. I think the reason Korean professional golfers are weak at international competitions is because it is difficult to practice in the winter and their rhythm is broken. In the winter, you will need to maintain your stamina more than your score and continue playing without losing your sense of rhythm to prepare for full-scale play in the spring.

D. Golf on the Mountain course

Golf courses built on the beach are called seaside courses or links. Representative examples include the Old Course in St. Andrews, Scotland, the birthplace of golf, and the Pebble Beach Golf Links Course in California, USA.

There are many mountainous areas in Korea and most golf courses were created by carving out the mountains, so they have the characteristics of mountainous courses with high altitude. Compared to flat courses on a continent as wide as the United States, Korea's courses require accurate shots and are also courses that require stamina.

Not only is the distance between holes long, but there are many dogleg courses where the green or flagpole is not visible from the teeing ground. In most cases, one side of the course is high, so it is advantageous to hit the ball toward a high slope rather than hitting it straight. There are times when you have to find the place where the ball landed in the wrong place.

In addition, in some places, the golf course was created by cutting the mountain steeply, so it is difficult to find the ball when the OB is hit by forming a cliff, and even if the OB is not hit, there are many cases where you have to hit from the slope, which results in a significant loss of distance in these cases.

In comparison, since the bunker is artificially created rather than natural terrain, it is not very deep, so it is not that difficult to hit a shot from the bunker.

Originally, the grass was in poor condition and difficult to maintain due to the stuffy military environment, but nowadays, lawn management has been managed and the grass is well maintained even on the new course.

However, the reality is that the grass fades in the fall and winter, which greatly hinders play, and in extreme cases, tee play is recommended, reducing the enjoyment of golf by half.

There is a big difference compared to southern countries where the weather is warm, where golf courses remain green all year round and beckon golfers. That's why a lot of people go abroad to play these days.

In addition, beach greens are relatively soft, making it difficult for balls to stop or cause backspin, whereas greens in Korea tend to be dry except for summer, making it easy for balls to roll.

Additionally, there are many greens where the green is generally higher than the fairway, so you need to take this into consideration when adjusting the distance when making your approach.

If there is a mountain on one side and the sea on the other, the line of the green is slanted towards the sea, making putting quite difficult. However, on greens.

In Korea, which are surrounded by mountains on all sides, you can successfully putt if you read the lines well. Some of the courses in our country are too steep, so it is difficult for older people or lady golfers with relatively less energy to play in the middle of summer. Not only that, but on uphill holes on mountain courses, clubs are used with a longer distance than the indicated distance, and on downhill holes, clubs are used with a longer distance than the indicated distance. Conversely, since a short club must be used, a person who has frequently played on the course and is familiar with the distance has a relative advantage.

In addition, the direction and strength of the wind is not constant for each hole with different elevations, and once the fog comes in, in severe cases, the fog does not clear up until almost 11 a.

m, making it impossible to play.

Therefore, it is necessary to play while considering appropriate strategies and measures in preparation for these various cases. Only then can you enjoy playing and improve your skills.

E. Logics of skill occupying 30%

Somehow, I hit it so well yesterday that I got a great score, but today, even if I hit it well, not only does it end up in the bunker or the rough, making it difficult to hit the ball, but I hit it well and thought I was on, but the ball got stuck on the edge at the back of the green and I putted downhill. As we face this, it becomes more and more mountainous.

But the opponent thought the tee shot was sliced and going OB to the right, but didn't it hit a tree and return to the fairway? I hit it with a fairway wood, and it fell a little short of the green, but it rolled right up to the edge of the green.

No matter how well I hit a downhill putt, I only get 3 putts, but my opponent ends up with 2 putts when going uphill. I sigh to myself, wondering if this is the only skill I have after 10 years of golf experience. No, it's 7 luck and 3 skill. While masturbating, I move to the next hall.

In fact, I hit my tee shot and approach shot flawlessly, but on some days, I had a hard time getting into a bunker by a narrow margin or being out of bounds, and there were one or two putts that didn't go in slightly past the hole. Is it bun? How can it be controlled by human power?

So, whenever that happens, we soothe ourselves or comfort the other person with 'luck 7 technique 3 reasoning'.

If you watch TV, the ball you approach may miss the hole slightly, or in extreme cases, it may go in and then come out. Can we say that it goes in if you hit it well, and doesn't go in if you hit it wrong?

However, when I think about it calmly, I think the '7 luck and technic 3 argument' is an exaggeration. Attributing 70% to luck and at most 30% to skill can be seen as degrading golf as a healthy sport.

Of course, there are cases where results are difficult to predict with human effort, but amateurs who do not practice and improve their skills and attribute the day's bad score to luck can be seen as cute. However, if you mistakenly believe that golf itself ends with '7 luck, 3 skills, and 3 arguments', you may neglect skill improvement and mental cultivation, which may hinder its development as a healthy sport.

There are things people know instinctively from the time they are born, there are things they learn and know, and there are things they know through effort and effort.

Compared to appetite and sexual desire, which you learn instinctively, or various studies that you learn, sports such as horse racing, bicycle racing, bowling, billiards, basketball, and volleyball allow you to improve your skills by sweating and practicing hard. If we put it into the previous three categories, we can say that golf belongs to the third category that requires effort and effort.

Therefore, since it is a skill in golf that you can raise your score by improving your skills through repeated practice, and by doing so, your score can be improved, I think the best thing to do is to constantly improve your golf technique without hoping for a fluke. Wouldn't it be the right way to go home today, vowing to improve my golf skills and turn things around with 3 Luck and 7 Skills?

15. Exodus

The Jewish people, led by Moses, set out to find the land of hope. Afterwards, repeating history countless times, the poor and downtrodden people set out to find new horizons. Today, when the entire Earth family has become one, the breath of liberation is rippled everywhere like the rising tide.

Waves of people seeking freedom. Among them are people who play golf. People who have been confined at home and bound by tradition for hundreds of years come out into the fields with golf clubs in hand.

A place where traditions break down and new breath breathes. First men, and now women, came forward and destroyed the old order and existing authority.

This wave of freedom spreads infinitely outwards, riding the wave of internationalization and globalization, not only within the country but also to the warm southern countries and the vast continent.

A. Popularization of golf

Looking at the golf driving ranges that are mushrooming compared to the decreasing number of tennis courts, the enthusiastic beginners and housewives in their 30s who come out to practice from 5 a. m and the difficulty in booking not only on weekends but also during the week, it feels like we are in the golden age of golf.

Golf, which was thought to be played only by the privileged on a few golf courses just 20 to 30 years ago, has recently become popular and has developed into a national sport due to several factors. First, as income increased and people had more time to spare, many people began picking up golf clubs.

Second, the development of transportation due to the spread of passenger cars has facilitated leisure sports activities.

Third, with the increase in income and the development of national consciousness, women were liberated from the home, allowing them to go out to the sea, mountains, and health centers. Golf also played a part. In particular, as middle-aged women have more free time as they are relieved from raising children, more and more people are choosing golf as an exercise.

Fourth, golf, which was previously only implicitly allowed for company executives and high-ranking executives, has spread to lower-level executives in the workplace, and young people in their 20s and 30s have come to make up the majority of the golf population. Under the corporate management system through autonomous competition and the information revolution, the existing authoritarian mindset of executives is gradually disappearing and authority is transferred to lower levels, and the mentality of learning golf at an early age is spreading.

Of course, in addition to this, the increase in incentives for golf due to the development of mass media, the extreme tendency to develop it early if you have talent, and the development and popularization of golf equipment are on par with the development of tourism, and now it is possible to travel not only domestically but also overseas and anywhere in the world. You can also trace the footsteps of Korean golfers.

This is the golden age of golf. However, the popularization of golf was inevitably accompanied by a decline in the quality of golf, resulting in so-called vulgarization. Golf, which has been recognized as a gentlemanly sport, seems to be transforming into a symbol of power, a show of wealth, and a byword for disorder, which is truly pitiful.

Chapter 1 of the Golf Rules stipulates etiquette because a true game is only possible when manners and etiquette are combined with technique. However, the increase in behaviors such as shouting, gambling, and swearing at caddies on the golf course can also be said to be a side effect of popularization.

In order to prevent the popularization of golf from deteriorating its quality, golfers must exercise restraint and follow the rules to make it a true sport. At the same time, they must learn the true meaning of golf and study techniques and strategies to play golf in accordance with its original purpose. This is an urgent matter.

B. The golfer's path

It is common for a golfer to cry over a slice at first, and the more he tries to correct the slice, the more his form becomes messed up, resulting in a slice form.

In my impatience to hit a long hit as quickly as possible, the coach gives me some corrections, but when I go out on the field, I slice again and go to the right, into the mountains, and I wonder why. However, it is a matter of degree, and slices occur when it is crucial, so it is difficult to break down the 90 wall and collapses.

Then one day, the ball suddenly starts to go to the left, and the slice that I was so worried about starts flying in the direction of the hook, causing me a new worry.

In the meantime, I tried closing the club, changing the grip to a finger grip, and changing the swing from inside to out, but I was wondering what caused the slice and the hook ball again, and I looked through books and books. I try to correct it by looking at it, but is it that easy?

However, for some reason, I broke 90 once or twice, and because I made a bogey play, I was so happy that I went to work and boasted that I had broken 90.

However, the following Sunday, I worked hard to break 90 again, but I couldn't help but feel embarrassed when I ended up hitting 95-96 instead of 90, so I wondered how many holes I had three over par.

I had the desire to hit the ball well to the side of the green with a pitching wedge and get a par, so the ball I hit lightly hit the ground and stayed at 2-3m, and then the ball I hit in a hurry went behind the green and ended up three-putting. I said. No matter how well you hit your tee shot or your second shot, if you make a mistake around the green, you can easily end up with a double bogey, not to mention a bogey, and your score will not decrease.

In the meantime, I practiced some short irons at the driving range and thought I was getting it right to a certain extent, but when things got like this, I picked up a pitching wedge and practiced at a closer distance again, but I was disappointed with the limited time of 1 hour and 30 minutes, so I tried to pick up a driver and fix my slice, and before I knew it, I couldn't do it. Because I don't have enough time, I end up giving up on the approach shot. However, after breaking 100, there were many cases of hitting 90, and recently I occasionally broke 90, but I didn't know that hitting 80 was that difficult.

In the meantime, I went on an overseas business trip and was busy with work, so I didn't have time to practice, so I played a few times with my friend on the weekends, but my score didn't seem to have decreased after that, so I got nervous. However, compared to before, there are fewer OBs or roughs due to slices, and there are fewer three-putts, so it seems to have improved, and in golf, scores go up and down like the stock market.

My friend, a so-called single with over 10 years of experience, doesn't seem to have much distance, but he finished with an approach and a putt and hit the 80s. I missed one or two holes, but a triple bogey was the decisive factor, so I couldn't reduce my score, so I'll wait for the next time.

As time goes by, I now hit the 80s a lot, and when I look at my score card, the numbers 87 and 88 sometimes appear, so I ask myself how much money I have invested so far.

My friend is always 3 or 4 points ahead of me

these days, so I get even more excited than before, wondering if it makes sense that I'm in my early 80s now and can't break 80. I bought a book, a membership, and encouraged my wife, who had worked hard all this time, to start playing golf. Everyone in my family seems to be obsessed with golf, so we make plans to go to Jeju Island or even Guam on vacation. Truly, a golfer's life is busy.

C. Who called 'golf widow'

Is golf really a sport that is so fun and worthy of passion that one can indulge in it twelve months a year, regardless of the four seasons: spring, summer, fall, and winter, without taking care of household chores? Although golf has been introduced to Korea a long time ago, it has not been that long since it became widely available to the general public. As the national income increased, life became richer, time became more available, automobiles became widespread, and the range of activities expanded, the golf boom began, and we can say that we have entered the era of popularization of golf.

However, among the various changes brought about by golf, both past and present, the change in family life is probably the biggest.

Wouldn't it be surprising if the term 'golf widow' was even used in the English–speaking world, the home of golf?

It is certain that once you start playing golf, you will have less time to take care of household chores. Considering the current traffic congestion, not only does it take 7 to 8 hours to get to the golf course, including 4 hours round trip and 5 hours of playing time, but if you play with friends, you can't help but have a drink, so weekend golfers who spend their long–awaited weekend outside are looking like children. How many times can I see this in a month? The whole family is suffering from high school disease, but the head of the family goes out, saying he doesn't know about me and says it's business, so the housewife, who is not a widow in her 30s or 40s, can't help but be annoyed.

So these days, on weekdays when their husbands are at work, the majority of housewife golfers are at the driving range, and most of the weekday reservations on the field are made up of female golfers, so it feels like the era of women's golf is at the top. Who said 'golf widow'

However, the purpose seems to be slightly different in Korea and foreign countries.

In the case of Europe and America, despite its long history, there do not seem to be many female amateur golfers. In countries with a well-established social security system, there are many retired and retired elderly people on golf courses, and young women are not seen in many places, but in Korea, there are many young women, which shows a significant improvement in the status of Korean women.

In the United States, if you go to most country clubs, you can see a lot of elderly people paying cheap fees to play, but it is not common for young women to play. In fact, the number of Korean men and women who come there to play golf has increased noticeably recently.

Perhaps that's why, among women, there are amateur golfers who can hit as well as men, while there are also many golfers who hit the ball so hard that it falls right in front of their noses as well as their form.

Most of these female golfers, unlike men, are born with women's unique physical conditions and relatively weak stamina, so not only do they lose distance, but their swing motion is also an upright swing rather than a flat swing. It is a characteristic.

Alternatively, he uses more fairway wood than iron to adjust the distance, and due to his delicate nature, he often tops, but on the other hand, his excellent putting sense is a great help in reducing his score.

Also, unlike men, most female golfers do not focus on scores, but rather enjoy the sport and often hang out with classmates, mothers' associations, younger siblings, and neighbors out of a sense of freedom.

While men are tied to work and enjoy weekends, women use weekdays, so not only are they relatively free to make reservations, but they can also increase the frequency if they have the financial means, so talented housewives can compete with men on regular schedules. It can be said that it is a natural trend that the number of talented players who are not inferior in scores is increasing.

This is not unrelated to the fact that Korean women have recently been able to stand out in the world of professional golf, creating new prospects. It feels like it is becoming a women's golf paradise.

D. Motivation for entering golf

In the 1970s, before golf became popular, a businessman went out to the field and got a long-awaited opportunity to play a round for the first time in his life. However, for some reason, his tee shot from the teeing ground of the first hole did not hit the ball, but he kept missing the ball once, twice, three times. The fact that there were many players waiting behind him also caused psychological anxiety, but when it happened not once, but twice or three times, the fellow player couldn't stand it anymore and said, "You're just blowing the wind." and made fun of him.

The person who was known for being quiet had never done any exercise other than hiking, and he came to the field without any prior practice, so there was no way he would have hit the ball.

But this is no laughing matter. This is a phenomenon that can still be seen occasionally these days, and it can be said to be a case where a player comes out without prior practice in the mood of having fun, and then their face becomes colorless.

There may be various situations for beginners who start playing golf, but people who have consistently played sports such as baseball or tennis seem to quickly master golf.

In general, balls have similar properties, so people who are good at baseball or tennis are also good at golf, and it may be natural that people who start playing in their 40s or 50s without time to enjoy such leisure activities have a hard time.

The reason Randle, a world-renowned tennis player, debuted on the golf stage and became a professional, and the reason why these famous athletes appear in social matches and still maintain good scores is because ball sports have something in common.

In that respect, people who are working and do not have sufficient time or financial resources should first improve their body's flexibility by using the leisure sports facilities provided by each workplace.

I was amazed to see several tennis enthusiasts I know who, as soon as they started playing golf, mastered it several times faster than others and hit the 80s within a year.

Also, these days, it has become difficult to speak uniformly as young students go to the practice range with their parents in the hope of becoming professional golfers in the future, while housewives eagerly swing golf clubs to enjoy their leisure time while their children are at school.

The problem is that the psychological conflict one experiences when playing golf without basic physical training is that great.

When you start playing at the age of 40 to 50, some of you are a self-shamer who always feels self-destructive compared to fellow golfers who started more than 10 years before you, or a hard worker who visits the practice range every morning and evening when you have the opportunity to see your skills improving day by day. These people, including the wealthy who take turns buying and testing the latest drivers that appear in golf magazines because they can't hit the distance, can be said to be a cross-section of amateur golfers who started late but are trying to reduce their scores.

Golf is something that is hard to back off once you get into it, so the fun of golf lies in the determination to master it quickly and play better than those who started before you. It's something to start with and see what will happen.

E. Passion for Golf

Since the motivation for starting golf is different for each person and the time and environment in which they started playing is different, it can be said that the passion for golf is also different.

When early golfers go out to the field with a golf club, they are usually excited from early in the morning, wondering how they will hit today and achieve good results.

Then, as you gradually become accustomed to golf and your scores improve, and you become more confident in competing with others, you will either make a bet for lunch or dinner, or go out on the field to make sure to win back the game you lost last time.

When playing golf, different personalities emerge during the course of 18 holes, so would you say that a seasoned golfer doesn't rush and waits for his opponent to collapse? On the other hand, high-handicapped golfers are unable to control their minds well and usually end up self-destructing.

As with all sports, the greatest joy of a game lies in winning, so it goes without saying that the joy of winning is greater than that of losing. However, when dealing with a long–awaited friend or a new stranger, the focus is on manners and skills rather than winning, so if you become too obsessed with winning, you may end up doing something that is rude to the other person. Even more so when it comes to hospitality golf? However, even in the Olympics, where participation is more important than victory, there are times when various methods are used to achieve victory, which is frowned upon. In the end, all games may exist to win. If not, isn't there a need to develop your skills and sharpen your energy?

In golf, where etiquette is emphasized and you have to check yourself while playing, the joy of winning while following the rules is even more special. In order to achieve that kind of victory, you work hard, and one day, when your score breaks 100, 90, and finally 80, you feel ecstatic as if you have finally become part of the golf world.

Not only do you find yourself sweating on your tanned face under the hot sun in the summer or on a cold winter day, wearing layers of clothes and swinging your body around to find a ball in the rough, but sometimes you don't mind criticism from society and go on an overseas expedition and stay away from home for a few days. In some cases, is golf really that much fun?

Anyway, after playing 18 holes under the hot summer sun, when you go to the bathroom to take a shower and take a bath, it is normal for everyone to feel the same joy after a day's work, whether they played well or not.

It can also be a social gathering place when you feel refreshed, relax your body and mentality, and sip a beer with a light heart, recheck your scores, and naturally talk about your sons and daughters and business with each other. And then secretary announces the results calling the name, everyone is happy if they receive a runner-up, nearest, longest, or even a lucky prize even if they do not win, and the winner who is called last gets the trophy along with the joy of winning. He holds it high, giving thanks to people, is the highlight of the enjoyment of amateur golf.

When you release all your stress like this, make plans for the next time, and head home, you return to the secular world and drive on the highway.

16. Place de la Concorde

A place where people of all ages and genders gather together. There, people meet new people, talk to each other, and offer opinions. This forum for dialogue that transcends generations creates harmony and tolerance, and ultimately brings peace.

People naturally become friends when they meet. It was a long time since we last met. A place where the compatriots who were separated by the mountains, cut off by water, and separated into the north, south, east, and west drove their cars and drove on the road at dawn when caves were opened and bridges were built to pave the way.

That place is the backcountry of the past, the golf course of today. There, I meet old friends I haven't seen in a long time, meet colleagues, and unwind. Now the nation is one, and the path to unification will also open here

A. young man's golf

If you are playing with the same handicapper, a young person cannot beat an older person with some experience. If a young golfer who has just started playing golf plays bogey and plays with an older golfer who is also a bogey player, the more experienced golfer will often win.

The young man is full of spirit and sometimes flies 230m and sometimes catches a birdie, but he often goes OB once or twice and ends up in the rough, and when he gets on the green, he often two-putts or three-putts. An older player with a lot of experience not only has almost no OB even if he doesn't go far, and even if he gets into the rough, he doesn't panic and easily moves to a good place to hit the next green.

One is an ambitious player, and the other plays calmly over and over again, but in golf, which requires patience, a calm golfer can be said to have an advantage.

If you look at the scores after playing all 18 holes, most of the older players do not have much difference in scores between the out and in courses, so it is often 43 in the first half and 47 or 45 in the second half, or 45, while young people score 42 in the first half and 48 or 44 in the second half. There are many cases where the difference in score becomes large, such as 46, and in extreme cases, 40 may be added to 50, resulting in an increase of about 10 points. The score difference shows that, even for the same bogey player, young golfers who focus on long shots generally have severe ups and downs because their strength is not yet refined.

However, being able to hit 40 in 9 holes implies the possibility of hitting 40 in 9 holes at some point, so it can be said that young people have an advantage in terms of potential ability.

If the two compete again in a year, there is a high probability that the younger one will improve. Accordingly, in golf today, not only the final score is important, but also the process must be analyzed and used as a reference for future play, and attention must also be paid to studying hitting techniques to prevent mishits.

While older golfers maintain their scores by solving an already established swing form with experience and their own hitting methods, young golfers are still in the process of learning and their hitting methods are not set in stone, so they can reduce their scores as much as they want depending on how much effort they make.

In addition, there is hope because by utilizing the vitality of young people, we can constantly absorb new batting methods and information to bring about technological improvement and development.

Therefore, when you get a taste for progressive golf and golf that constantly challenges you, golf becomes more fun and interesting.

B. Golf across generations

Most amateur golfers in Korea started playing golf when they reached middle age. Instead of steady building up their skills from the basics at a young age, they began picking up golf clubs after the 1980s, as people's living standards improved and the number of cars and golf courses increased, and the number increased dramatically.

Depending on the person, some people start in their 40s or 50s, while others start in their 30s, so there are not many people who start after their muscles and bones have hardened and have a proper swing form or hitting technique.

Then, when you enter your 50s and become a senior, the reality is that you no longer have the strength and energy to correct it, so you usually enjoy golf with a firm form and make the most of your leisure time.

In comparison, many recent golfers started playing when they were young, and since teaching methods have changed significantly, the number of golfers who play using a principled swing form is increasing.

However, the reality of amateur golfers is that they do not contribute significantly to improving their scores because they try to play with a focus on power rather than technique around the green, and remain at high handicap levels.

In the 1960s or early 1970s, when seniors first started playing golf, there were not many golf driving ranges, few instruction books, and videos were not developed, so there were few opportunities to receive lessons.

However, today, with the opening of doors and the flow of various cultures, it is not only easier to learn, but also various systems and facilities have improved a lot compared to then, and learning can be done at a younger age, so opportunities are much greater.

However, since most amateur golfers started playing golf as a leisure activity simply for enjoyment, most golfers who started playing in the last 4 to 5 years are quick golfers, and there are not many golfers who have built up solid skills after basic training.

On the contrary, due to the rapid increase in the golf population in a short period of time, it has caused confusion in the golf order, resulting in various side effects such as difficulty in booking, lax compliance with golf rules, and poor golf progress, which has been criticized.

Considering the fact that golf has developed into a sport managed by the players themselves, it can be said that now is the time to hone one's skills and observe manners and etiquette that ensure orderly play.

C. Chaebol CEO's Golf

The heads of Korean conglomerates, especially those of the second generation, also stand out in golf, with many of them being single-digit handicappers or low handicappers hitting the 80s, making it seem like there is a functional relationship between business and golf.

In general, business owners were busy with work during the early stages of Korea's economic development in the 1960s and 1970s and did not have time to enjoy golf. However, the second generation of chaebol's devoted themselves to golf during their school days and studying abroad, greatly improving their skills, with some becoming single-handy golfers. It seems that ordinary employees can't help but feel nervous as they do business with such ferocity.

Accordingly, most of the employees of conglomerates who understand golf and own golf courses enjoy golf freely and improve their skills, while employees of companies that do not have golf courses and whose CEO does not play golf cannot freely go to the golf course, resulting in differences between companies.

However, due to the rapid expansion of the golf population in the past several years and changes in the new Generation
However, due to the rapid expansion of the golf population in the past 2-3 years and due to changes in their job views, golf as a means of leisure is continuing to increase.

Moreover, recently, as the import of various golf equipment has been liberalized and tariffs have been reduced, the number of people holding new golf clubs has increased, gradually differences in color between companies have disappeared and skills have become equalized, and individual skill differences have become more noticeable.

In addition, in the future, it is expected that the younger generation will give up the concept of a lifelong job and tend to not only choose a job according to their hobbies but also freely choose leisure activities, and so the number of people who prefer golf will continue to spread.

On the other hand, recently, as the number of

CEOs and employees of small and medium—sized companies who are becoming independent rather than being closely tied to large corporations as in the past has increased, their golf skills have improved significantly, and golf is now moving away from being an exclusive sport for conglomerates. You can also do it.

However, considering the current situation of golf's booking difficulties and the fact that Korea's large corporations have a monopolistic competitive advantage in the market, the connection between chaebols and golf cannot be denied for the time being.

D. President's golf

A book containing the golf anecdotes of 13 of the 16 U. S. presidents from President Taft in 1909 to President Clinton, excluding Presidents Hoover, Truman, and Carter, was published in the United States and is said to be garnering attention.

According to the book, President Eisenhower was a famous golf enthusiast who played 800 rounds during his eight—year term, averaging about two rounds per week.

President Kennedy was born into a wealthy

family, started picking up clubs in his teens, and was a single-handy golfer with a handiness of 7 to 10, enough to participate as a representative in a competition against Yale University during his freshman year at Harvard University. In particular, President Kennedy is said to have been good at hitting the 7-iron shot and used a smooth swing.

When President Nixon was vice president, he teamed up with President Eisenhower to participate in the competition and lost. After that, he devoted himself to practice and achieved a hole-in-one record in 1961.

President Reagan's handiness dropped to 12 when he was an actor, but it is said that he played less golf while in office.

President Bush is a handyman of 11. He is said to have played so fast that he earned the nickname 'speed golfer' and once played 18 holes in 1 hour and 42 minutes.

President Clinton is a long hitter with a driver shot that goes as far as 275 yards. However, it is said that he is an enthusiast in his late teens who is handy and can play slowly, sometimes taking more than 5 hours for one round.

In our country, even presidents who play golf amidst their busy political lives refrain from playing golf during their term, so there is no official data to prove this. In particular, one of the current president expressed he would not to travel on business during his term, creating a contrast with the United States.

When the President goes out to the golf course, security is high to ensure security and identity, and the front and back holes are often empty. There is also a saying that ordinary people play 'presidential golf' when they play leisurely and the front and back holes are empty.

However, because the playing time is usually about 4 hours, many golfers end up finishing only 9 holes, so even the President may not be able to play golf as leisurely as he wants. In particular, in recent years, the number of golfers has increased rapidly, making it difficult for even the President to play leisurely, and the opportunity for ordinary people to play so-called 'Presidential golf', which is played with empty front and back holes, is decreasing. Would it be a pity that opportunities for the general public to play so-called Presidential golf', played with empty front and back holes, are decreasing?

17. Medical Bible Donguibogam

An immortal medical monument compiled by medical doctor Heo Jun, Donguibogam.

A person's five organs and six parts are within it, and the cure for all diseases is contained therein.

If you master the principles of heaven above and realize human nature below and put them into practice, you can preserve your health and enjoy a hundred years of life. Otherwise, you will become the source of all diseases. People are inherently stupid.

The self-proclaimed lord of all creation who cannot rest even though he overworks his body all day long and squeezes his five organs and six pertusion the jungle of buildings, the bodies and minds are exhausted on the hard asphalt, and the backs and legs are weakened by the swivel chairs, but the animals are moving around busily. You now need to take a break ⋯

A. In the shade house

It is difficult to play golf without strong physical strength to continue playing for about 4 to 5 hours.

So, when we arrive at the clubhouse, we usually order a simple meal, such as hangover soup, gomtang, beef stew or loach stew, and egg flies, and eat them up before tee-up time.

This is inevitable. If you leave home around 4 or 5 am and arrive at the golf course around 6:30 or 7 am, there are many times when you have not eaten breakfast, so you eat breakfast first and then go around the course to quench your hunger.

That's not all, even if you reserve a tee-up time around 12 or 2 PM on Saturday, there are many cases where you hurriedly eat lunch at the clubhouse and then head out to the first hole.

Also, if you usually play for 4 to 5 hours, there is often a lunch break in the middle, so you often eat while going around the course or after finishing the out-course.

If you don't have much time, stop by the shade house on the course and have a light meal.

In such cases, it is usually after a meal, so the tee shot ball is not hit properly and often becomes a ground ball, slice, or hook.

The food you suddenly eat affects your body, causing subtle changes that affect your stroke. So, we sometimes experience that a shot that was hit well until then becomes temporarily shaky.

Among various types of exercise, there are very few that require eating during exercise, but since golf takes 4 to 5 hours, you cannot continue exercising unless you satisfy your hunger before or in the middle, so you usually end up eating.

The amount of food eaten at this time varies from person to person, so it cannot be stated in unilateral terms, but it is common to choose and eat what suits one's taste.

The problem is that because of these meals, you sometimes miss the ball when you hit it right after eating. What should you do about this? A Korean athlete went on an expedition to Southeast Asia and competed on a starving stomach. After getting a poor score, he realized that exercise would not work well without a hungry spirit. From then on, he adjusted his food appropriately to achieve good results. He once said that he was able to reap it.

Physiologists say that food is not digested immediately after eating, but usually takes about one to two hours to be digested, strengthening one's physical strength. Therefore, it can be said that while digestion is in progress, it puts a burden on the stomach and has a slight impact on the sense of movement.

Since amateur golf is played for the purpose of socializing and entertainment rather than being played with a thorough professional spirit, some people rather enjoy eating as a hobby and want to fill up the game rather than obsess over golf, which is not suitable for them.

In England and America, it is common to not even be able to see a shade house while playing 18 holes. Shade houses seem to be exclusive to Korea and Japan.

On days when you normally strengthen your stamina and strengthen your body to play, it is polite to support your fellow players indirectly by playing seriously. Even if it is said that sightseeing is after a meal, golf is not an sightseeing but is a sports. If you're going to exercise, shouldn't you control your food appropriately?

B. Golf and leg strength

Golf, like other sports, is a sport that presupposes strong legs. First of all, the fairway, which requires 4–5 hours of walking, is 6–7 km long, and considering the distance between holes and the occasional hook and slice, 10 km is enough. If you go on a steep mountain course, it's much more difficult.

Moreover, when you do not simply walk but make a swing motion to hit the ball, you have to place both feet firmly on the ground and twist your waist to exert telekinesis, so if your legs are weak, you will sway or one foot will fall. Because it is lifted, it lacks the strength to squeeze out telekinesis, making it impossible to move a sufficient distance.

Of course, there are many cases where the swing form is immature at first and the swing cannot be performed properly, but there are also many cases where the swing cannot be performed properly due to lack of foot strength and shaking legs.

Therefore, to swing properly, you need to strengthen your feet and legs.

Just as Ernie Els from South Africa strengthened his body through weightlifting and

Fred Couples strengthened his body by starting out as a baseball player, amateurs also need to strengthen their feet and leg strength to play golf properly.

Most modern people commute by car rather than walking and work while sitting in an office, so it is common for their legs to weaken without realizing it.

Also, the first parts that become weak, as we age, seem to be our legs and eyes. Even in golf, it is difficult to show off your skills if these two parts are weak, so it is important to train your basic physical strength by jogging, riding a bicycle, or going up and down stairs.

Compared to the feet and legs, the strength of the arms and hands does not seem to require much relative strength. As the golf swing rotates the waist and shoulders, the arms and hands follow suit and swing the club, so it is necessary to maintain a firm grip, rhythm, and tempo, but if more force is applied, the balance is usually broken.

It is often seen that people with strong wrists swing using only their hands, resulting in a change in the overall swing.

The hands and arms can be said to fulfill

their function if they have rhythmic elasticity and transmit the torque coming from the waist and shoulders to the club.

Therefore, in order to maintain strong legs, or healthy legs, it is most important to do appropriate exercise on a daily basis.

C. Golf and back pain

The golf swing is a type of un-balancing exercise in which the swing is performed by twisting the waist while keeping both feet on the ground and using telekinesis to bounce back.

Therefore, many people complain of back pain due to excessive stress placed on their back while playing golf hard, and most people will have experienced pain once or twice.

Among professional golfers, world famous stars Jack Nicklaus and Fred Couples have suffered from back pain, and many professional golfers in Korea are said to be suffering from back pain.

There was a report that Corey Pavin, who participated in the SsangRyong Challenge competition many years ago, complained of back pain during the second round and performed somewhat worse than the previous day, but after receiving treatment that night, he was on his way to victory the next day.

Typically, when a young golfer hits hundreds of balls a day to achieve great success, the stress caused by the aforementioned unbalance builds up in his lower back, causing pain one day, and when the pain is severe, he becomes unable to swing the golf club properly. It seems to be more common in men than in women.

In addition to the back, some people complain of problems with their shoulders and ribs, while others complain of finger pain, but back pain seems to be the most common case.

Therefore, to prevent this, it is necessary to practice by controlling the time appropriately rather than hitting the ball intensively in one or two hours. It is also important to learn natural swing movements to avoid putting too much strain on your body. It is not a good idea to imitate John Daly to achieve a somewhat longer distance or to practice with only a driver every day.

In addition, after hitting a practice ball or playing a round, it is a good idea to properly relieve body fatigue and prepare for tomorrow.

If you relieve your fatigue in the bath after exercising and pay attention to using appropriate yoga techniques to relieve back fatigue when you return home, you will be able to prevent this in advance.

D. Golfer wearing glasses

When you watch the PGA Tour in the United States on TV, it seems like there aren't many players wearing glasses except for the famous player Tom Kite years ago.

Meanwhile, on the senior tour, only Bob Charles wears glasses, but overall he does not wear glasses, which shows that his eyesight is relatively good, and only with good eyesight can you achieve good results in golf.

Of course, not only golf but all sports cannot achieve good results if you have poor eyesight, and the paradoxical conclusion is that while sports played outside in the fresh air, such as golf, are good for your health, they are especially good for your eyes.

However, among amateur golfers who do not play golf full-time, there are quite a few who started playing golf while wearing glasses due to poor eyesight.

In golf, the tee shot direction is determined by determining whether there is an obstacle 200 to 250 meters ahead, and when approaching, an accurate distance measurement is required. Also, on the putting green, which is a score box, you must hit straight while looking at the putting line between the hole and the ball as well as the condition of the green. Because it is an physical exercise, vision is even more important. Another handicap related to vision is color blindness.

Although complete color blindness is rare, red—green color blindness accounts for a significant portion of the population, so many golfers are red—green color blind or have color blindness.

The biggest problem in such cases is that the position of the flagpole against the green bushes must be clearly visible, but it is difficult to distinguish the red flagpole buried in the green leaves, so there are times when you hit the ball without checking the direction.

In foreign countries, the green flagpole is colored white when it is in the middle of the green, red when it is further forward, and blue when it is behind the green, so that it can be used as a reference when approaching.

Therefore, you must know that healthy eyes are absolutely necessary to be an excellent golfer, and make efforts to protect your eyes on a daily basis. Also, I would like to add that if you play with such a handicap, you need more patience and effort.

end